Resurrection Update

Snow herd 182

still here
131

Upland
Birds
124

Almost
Noon
130

19

Anthropology
123

The mixture
probably doesn't
work but I like
it anyway

41

Avatar 176

√√ 131

Indirective
212

On Exploration
201

22

182

Materialism – 175

easy-out
endings not really
organic

172 – Grief's
aspect

James Galvin

Resurrection Update

COLLECTED POEMS · 1975–1997

COPPER CANYON PRESS

Publication of this book is supported by a grant from the National Endowment for the Arts and a grant from the Lannan Foundation. Additional support to Copper Canyon Press has been provided by the Washington State Arts Commission. Copper Canyon Press is in residence with Centrum at Fort Worden State Park.

Library of Congress Cataloging-in-Publication Data
Galvin, James
Resurrection update: poems 1975–1996 / by James Galvin.
p. cm.
ISBN 1-55659-121-7. – ISBN 1-55659-122-5 (pbk.)
1. Title.
PS3557.A444R47 1996
811'.54 – DC21   96-51285

COPPER CANYON PRESS

P.O. BOX 271, PORT TOWNSEND, WASHINGTON 98368

Contents

GOD'S MISTRESS (1984)

SALT

THE SPRUCE FOREST

HALF THE STARS

LETHAL FREQUENCIES (1995)

STATIONS (NEW POEMS) (1996)

Resurrection Update

Imaginary Timber

1980

IMAGINARY TIMBER

I

Notes for the First Line of a Spanish Poem

We remember so little,
We are certain of nothing.
We long to perish into the absolute.
Where is a mountain
To spread its snowfields for us like a shawl?

You might begin,
The men who come to see me are not exactly lovers.
Or, *Seen at a distance the gazelle is blue.*
That's just your way of cheering me up.

You might begin,
The quality of the telegram is vulnerable.
Or even, *The spirit of the telegram is virginal.*
By now I am ravenous.

You might begin,
Nothing's more passionate than a train,
Entering an enormous depot,
Empty except for two lovers, irreconcilable,
Parting. Then,
No one's more visible than a blind man on the street.

Things that are that were never meant to be!
Terrible music!

The utter confusion of surfaces!
The first steps toward probability!
You might begin,

Near the edge of the mind, the mind grows defenseless,
Sleepy in the way it sees,
Like Columbus on the edge of the world.
It feels the grip of all it cannot grasp,
Like the blind man trying to stay out of sight.
Show me any object, I'll show you rust on a wave.

You begin,

Outside the mind, the snow undresses and lies down.

News

These afternoons seem to occur more
In geologic time than in one's life.
Under the blue fresh snowfall,
Sandstone outcrops generate heat.
I count fifteen kinds of tracks,
Like runes, and nothing living.

Drifted snow, an ethered gauze,
Muffles the land, creaks under my skis,
Animals sleep among the roots,
Without doors, without dreams.
Seven miles for a phone
And even the wires have gone under.

Another day knowing nothing more
Than when I last saw you,
That stainless-steel shadow
Vigilant over your bed.
It followed you down the hospital halls,
Arms hung with surgical fruit.

I slide down the last drift to the house,
Slap my skis together.
A small avalanche, shaped like a continent,
Drifts off the roof and falls into a heap,
And some chinking falls from the eaves.

We each inhabit our own
Small flesh, our tract.
Each tries to keep his own

Doors from creaking, like news,
As each night slams shut, and each dawn opens
Like a sudden flow of blood from the mouth.

Everyone Knows Whom the Saved Envy

It isn't such a bad thing,
To live in one world forever.
You could do a lot worse:
The sexual smell of fresh-cut alfalfa
Could well be missing somewhere.
Somewhere you'd give in to some impetuous unknown,
And then stand guilty, as accused, of self-love.
It's better not to take such risks.

It's not as if we had no angels:
A handful remained when the rest moved on.
Now they work for a living,
As windmills on the open range.
They spin and stare like catatonics,
Nod toward the bedridden peaks.
They've learned their own angelic disbelief.

The mountains still breathe, I suppose,
Though barely.
The prairie still swells under a few small churches.
They are like rowboats after the ship's gone down.
Everyone knows whom the saved envy.
Runoff mirrors the sky in alpine pastures;
Imagine how quickly one's tracks unbloom there.
This world isn't such a bad world.

At least the angels are gainfully employed:
They know where the water is,
What to do with wind.
I try not to think of those others,

Like so many brides,
So many owls made of pollen
Wintering in a stand of imaginary timber.

Something to Save Us

As far as we know there's nothing more to say
About being so small for our size,
Nothing, therefore, about parentage.

There's nothing to say about maritime sadness:
Immodest signals from unreachable islands,
Earthrise on the moon.

There's little to say about innocence:
We'd land on distant planets
Like flies on the anvil;

We'd abandon our unborn,
Those intervals crouched around us wherever we are.
We'd wish the self even smaller,

Though the self is already smaller
Than anyone suspects.
All we wanted was a roundness we could count on.

There's nothing to say about the history of resurrection,
The chronicles on incapacity,
Nothing about falsehood or humor.

We are like relatives after an execution:
We've said we are like our own worn clothes
Hung to dry without us;

We've said we are like the windows of our own house
Falling away all at once;
We take root in the sound of our own breaking.

If there were something more to say,
How would that save us –
Violets, parasol, easy rain?

Lines about the Recent Past

In the recent past,
Always mad or dreaming,
Diminished by even a little distance,
I resemble everyone.

Is the wind dying? Is the spade willing?
I don't ask.

In the recent past weather is obsessive.
The sun is something complete
That sometimes looks away.

On their own good strength the cattle return
From all the long days of giving up their flesh.
Is this how we travel to the heart,
Like pollen back from the air?

I just want to say,
The past and the stiletto are shy by design.
It's unlikely that I'm mistaken in this.

They enter in a way less honest than true.

So much lowering of eyes!
In the recent past is the sleep of humility.

It's easy to belong in the world.

There are angels in the snow where birds have landed.

The Snowdrift as a Wave

for my mother

Consider this hour, this death.
It leans toward me. We touch.
It has a fragrance like burning lace.

Pitchwood in the furnace:
The damned making love,
The drowned in their ships, tapping with wrenches.

The winter I was eight,
Snow drifted up twenty feet around our house.
We left the truck and snowshoed home.
Father brought his mother, bundled on my sled.

Had you stopped to rest,
To lean your arm against a tree?
Were you always so unhappy?

A sail billowing under the coals,
A seed waking in its pod.

I tunneled into that drift, made rooms,
Listened to the blizzard
As it made more waves like mine.
I had seen the sea once.

It opened its waves like drawers,
Repeating the name of something misplaced.
It searched the same drawers again and again.
It sounded like that snowstorm
Giving itself away.

Sadness

Tonight in the Southwest
Sadness is disappearing

Tonight in splash marks
On boulders

In the streambed
Sadness is disappearing

On mesas
In processions

Of miner's candles
Like Hohokam

Returning from the gulf
With salt

Tonight in the eyes
Of the oldest lion

Stirring our tracks
And in the heart

Of the cactus blossom
In the red spider

Knitting wheels
Humming to herself

In a voice like transparent thread
Sadness is disappearing

The maidenly lizard
In her sandstone room

In the dim light of a quartz lamp
Makes love to her shadow

Sadness is disappearing
Tonight in the desert

Like a drop of blood
On the map of the Southwest

And above us
A few in the dark audience

Smoking cigarettes

The Measure of the Year

A canoe made of horse ribs tipped over in the pasture.
Prairie flowers took it for a meetinghouse.
They grow there with a vengeance.

Buck posts float across the flooded swamp
Where my father rode in and under.
Different horse.

He held her head up out of the mud
And said how he was sorry
Till they came to pull him out.

We found the white filly
On the only hard ground by the south gate.
He said she'd been a ghost from the start and he was right.

We covered her with branches.
There were things he had the wrong names for
Like *rose crystals*. Though

They were about what you'd think from a name like that.
He told us somewhere on Sand Creek Pass
Was a crystal that spelled our own initials

And we should try to find it.
We walked through sagebrush and sand currents, looking.
He said pasqueflowers and paintbrush

Wait till Easter to grow,
Then they come up even with snow still on the ground.
I thought I'd seen that happen.

Airbrush

The sky was an occasion
I would never rise to. I had my doubts.

Frost fell back into morning shadows of things.
Gateposts and evergreens had two shadows then,
One white and twice as cold
With half the heart and half again
Smaller.

Better than expected was good enough.
A man could say *mercy* and mean it.

There were daughters in whom fathers
Would be well pleased, sons
Not able to breed, mothers among the living.

Fields blew away and blew back in, painless.
Everybody died since everybody does, still

I have my doubts
And they have shadows, double.

A Man's Vocation Is Nobody's Business

Overcome with humility in the American West,
Boys grew up incorruptible in old photographs.
In shirts without collars,
They stand next to the year's prize hog,
Thinking into the wind.

Taller than fathers or brothers,
The edges of kitchen doors
In sod houses
Recorded the ambitions of boys to grow

Tall enough to see more
Of the landscape as it took
Its turns for the worse.

From the top of a silo you could see
How the land had a hard time
Just holding up its fences,
Holding out for water, just holding
Back the sage and larkspur.

In eastern Colorado, old men and boys
Rode the fences together.
Once a year, in late summer,

They lifted the fence wires to the tops of cedar posts
For the tumbleweeds to blow under.

This is no secret.
The tumbleweed is a bristling genius
Bound for the edge of the world.

The Small Self and the Liberal Sky

Perhaps you didn't realize
Anything can happen under a sky like this.

Never give in to surprise:

Not for mountains
Who turn under sheets and breathe in
Each other's green scent;

Not for the lights where nobody lives;

Not for blood-colored mushrooms
That rise up one after one like little presidents;

Not for the small self, afraid
It has misunderstood the question.

Oh it's prepared to answer anyway,
It has its array of modest affirmations
Like anyone. Just that –

So many years and something in the leaves
Does not fall.

I find young starlings in the lake's ice,
Their wings spread like death-flowers pressed in a book;

Find moths spawned in the woodshed
Like a winter's supply of blossoms.

It's just that I was looking for a world
To walk into empty-handed.

That's when I found you, female, shamelessly
Sailing toward me in your folded paper boat.

Don't deny it, please.
At night the self feels smaller
And water is scarce in parts of the mind.

The small self is obliged, therefore,
To take back everything
Anyone has ever said.

No one is allowed to speak now
But you

IMAGINARY TIMBER

II

What I've Believed In

Propped on blocks, the front half of a Packard car rides the hillside like a chip of wood on the crest of a wave. It's part of the sawmill. That Packard engine runs it, or did. The rest, the belt, the Belsaw carriage and blade, stands aside in disrepair. Except for the pine seeds gophers have stashed in the tailpipe, there's no sign of anything living. The gull-wing hood is rusted cinnamon, latched over chrome priming cocks, one for each cylinder. Every board in every building here was milled on power from that old car, out of timber cut here too. Even shingles. It's been here since 1925, winters piling onto its forehead like a mother's hands. It's weathered them like a son. Just because it hasn't been run since 1956 is no reason to think it won't run now: waves have traveled thousands of miles to give us small gifts; pine seeds have waited years to be asked.

Snowlight

When my sister was small, Father carried her everywhere in a woven pack basket. Once he killed a deer with her strapped to his back. She moved and spoiled his first shot, and the deer ran off with one shattered hind leg. They ran two miles, stopping to shoot six times. My sister finally stopped screaming but she says her ears still ring.

My parents never said a word one way or another, but on the day before her husband died, my grandmother swears on the souls of saints she heard a banshee. Her sister, Ruth, heard it; but my sister and I were too young to be listening.

When she heard the cry, Grandmother was braiding a rug from colored rags and scraps of cloth. Her rugs began in the center and wound outward until they grew almost too large for rooms. They covered her lap and flowed to the floor, so that, to a child, she looked like the white peak of a mountain.

When Ruth shot herself, Father wrapped her body in one of my grandmother's rugs. When he returned from town, he hung the rug, like a salted hide, on the back fence. He left it there, between the tool shed and forge, for twenty years. Now it's little more than a spot on the fence, the gray boards bleached white.

Father says the worst thing is a windless December night with no moon, no stars, just snowlight glowing in through the windows, lighting the path to the springhouse. He says his ears ring so loud he can't sleep, and he thinks of the boot hammer in the shed, lying by the fenceposts; or the ring of steel on the anvil, someone forging hinges.

Without Saying

what a small sky for so much snow; what little snow for so much ground; what looks bigger when it's farther away; you could look across the land here and think there wasn't water for a hundred miles, not see the canyon. But you'd hear it if you were close, the water like a slow explosion. I threw my mother's ashes down there, and some of them rose, too, in the wind.

Every once in a while he likes to blow up something. He loads his coat pockets with dynamite sprouting fuses. Once he set charges under the outhouse. It went up in one piece and came apart as it came down. He would crimp blasting caps to fuses with his teeth, caps inside his mouth. Once he blew windows out of the house.

Winter mornings my mother went out with ashes from the stove. First the birds went up, juncos and jays, then the snow went up in the wind, and wood ashes went up from my mother's hand in the snow and birds, and she looked up too. Nothing goes without saying. Her hem was wet, her shawl was blue.

My father lies on top of his grave, waiting to go off, waiting for a rainstorm falling into the shape of a single tree. His hat is the cloud his head is in, blown through at the peak; the wind wants to be taken into consideration.

A Poem from Boulder Ridge

The skeleton of a teepee stood on Boulder Ridge in the winter of 1950. The first year Lyle wintered on Sheep Creek with his brothers, sister, and mother was 1937, and the dried elk hides still hung from the lodgepoles like the shirt of a starved man. A wind was eating his clothes. Rain licked the bones clean.

In the year I was born it fell and was covered by branches. By now it has sunk into the earth like goose down into snow.

A family of renegade Utes had left the reservation and come home to hunt where their fathers had taught them hunting. They died in the first winter, but I still feel them here, perhaps in the wood of an old ponderosa, their faces grown into pine boles: round-eyed, round-mouthed masks. Lyle's family is here too, who fell from him one after another.

Lyle's mother was a water witch for arrowheads. She showed the children where to look, near the petroglyphs on Sand Creek, or at Bull Mountain Spring. We found a few chips and scrapers, but the perfect points seemed to grow beneath her fingers as she stooped to pick them up. She peered into them and turned them over like names.

She said you have to listen to find a good arrowhead. It lies on top of the gravel and hisses with patience. You must look with eyes like flint. You pick it up, almost touching the hand that held it last, that gave it flight. You turn it over in your palm. It is like opening the door to a warm house. Someone is passing through it as if it were made for him, as if he made it.

Fathers and Indians

The mountain Utes who lived here burned these ridges to save them from settlement by whites. Like a jealous father who crops his daughter's hair to spare her the advances of vulgar young men, it was all they could do. It wasn't enough.

You can still see a few of the old trees, pitch-hardened, fire-hardened spars, standing dead and branchless for a hundred years. Once this whole country was covered with trees that size. They don't bend or break like living pines: the wind cracks and widens to let them in.

You can see them sometimes huddled together, sometimes alone like single masts in an ocean of spruce, sometimes high on open slopes in lines like somnambulists on a stair. A stair with too few steps, it doesn't reach.

Had they not been destroyed, they would not be remembered. The ones left standing remind us of the fallen, remind us there are forests of empty sleeves, tunneling into the sky.

Totem

Riding a '23 Farmall round and round on a hot afternoon, I always think of the dead spruce spar on the ridge behind the house. From here it pierces the skyline, asking for it, like a column of smoke. It must be a full hundred feet taller than anything living. But start up the hill and it disappears behind the smaller pines.

Why in all these years it hasn't caught a hot one and burned the whole mountain, God might have called an easy miracle. It stands bright against the sky, as if it had turned to quartz.

But I'd rather pull my hat down and watch the teeth of the hay rake making windrows, turning the meadow into a patch of corduroy, or see the iron wheels sink into the dough of the peat bog and imagine driving on the moon.

Each December I decide to cut it down. It takes till noon on snow-shoes just to top the ridge, where I climb a tree for a glimpse of the spar. I walk too long, climb another and see it somewhere else, as if the forest were moving it around.

I return home in the early dark. Perhaps I see some elk or a couple of fool hens. I decide death by fire is reassuring to a forest. This year I didn't try to find the snag. This year, everything that died, died twice.

Making Hay and Funerals

Sun comes late to the sheltered places. Any August morning she could have looked from her kitchen window, across garden rows, to the meadow. She'd have seen her son brushing frost from the tractor seat. She'd have seen his cigarette smoke suspended in air and might have thought the tractor like a barge, low in water, laboring upstream.

In winter four feet of snow could fall in a night. Any morning she could have watched the wind raising plumes into the air the way we used to believe the soul rises. Once the biggest elk they'd ever seen stood by the garden fence, wind ruffling his winter coat. The son took his rifle out to the porch. She saw the bullet hole snap open and stare.

All the neighbors came around for funerals and for haying. The women in the kitchen surrounded her like blankets. The men outside, standing or squatting in a circle, considered. After lunch, everyone seemed sleepy in the afternoon sun. Work was like a dream of work. The women wore bonnets, the men rolled cigarettes. Her husband, both her eldest sons, her only daughter: all their funerals were the same.

At night the men drank, traded songs or stories, and slept. She might have lain awake on any of those nights, listening to her last son's breathing. She might have told herself it would never stop and pulled the elk robe up over her ears. She might have remembered that collapse, how it was like an afterthought.

Homesteader

From the section mark back of the meadow, straight north to the river, the telephone lines and snakefence run together. The split rails cross as if they were prayerful. Deer jump over, gray wolves slide beneath.

In the kitchen a man lights a match. A basin of water with soap and whiskers keeps moths from the lamp flame. They paddle in circles and are faithful. There are places for these men, all the same man, to drift down alone: the tie hack, the water witch, the drover, the builder of houses according to stars.

Wind in the lodgepoles is like the good son who combs his mother's hair. She talks to him steadily: about the six-pound hammer in love with the anvil, about their issue of hinges; something about the grindstone, the telephone wire, snowshoe tracks to the river and traplines lost under ice. She tells him how we sing and cry, lie down in the distance and think we sleep.

Mouthpiece, earpiece, crank handle and wire, the phone reaches to the only other man in forty miles. By the end of December the line is down from the weight of snow or the elk walking through on high drifts. The snow leans in like bad advice, eyes take on a more distant shade, the stars brighten accordingly.

Every time it snows again it's like his body filling. A wire runs in and breaks under drifts. The man picks up the earpiece and listens. It clicks and rushes. The broken wire end is like a nerve in the snow. It's a conversation with the way things are.

Stringers for the Bridge

Wild mountain roses bloom in the ditches, the smell of sagebrush recurs. A single peak hovers to the north, barely visible. You have to believe in it to see it, and it *is* there: enough distance to make that difference. Small animals scatter like dice. Today we cut stringers for the bridge.

The chain saw gurgles, sputters, screams: we feed it. Ants still nest in the first tree's trunk. Cells in the body look like that, their contents mathematical and red. They bleed from the stump as I cut. They spill out and drench the chain and I press harder, as if I belonged.

I was nine when you first took me logging. We chose the straightest timber for the new barn. You taught me to use the short-handled ax, to keep it honed, to stand always on the side opposite the branches being trimmed. We went home early when a log rolled toward you and the chain saw notched your shin. You said you were OK, lucky, as we walked back to the truck and your boot filled.

Could I dig my toes into the years of needles and remain motionless long? These pine leaves fall into themselves a little confused. Like compass needles, each has an opinion of which way to go. How are they to know the map is already a wheel?

Utah Ghost Town

Not to mention what was written all over them, not to mention grief, which is our own invention, all these mining towns blew in on the same hot wind and settled over the Rockies like pages from the morning news. Here the graveyard folk are mostly children, whose deaths came early on in the stories of these towns.

There are deer tracks, leaf-shaped, on the graves, and aspen leaves in the lake's palm, like money. The sky is a doubtful umbrella above the hill where the graves are, unlike the umbrellas mothers twirled on Sunday visits.

Their children must have been like gold in the bottom of a well, for they dressed in black and stood by the graves – absolute windmills – yes, and all they saw high up were white wings, those flights of pelicans disappearing into the updrafts like bits of paper, blank. And all they saw beyond the hill was land till the sky comes down.

IMAGINARY TIMBER

III

As If.

I thought it took
A red-tailed hawk
To make hunger
Look so easy.
As if
It was your first time with me,
You lay awake all night,
Though your clothes
Went right to sleep
Like man's best friend
When you slipped
Into that other landscape.
As if the steam iron
Could dream
Of being a whale,
Becalmed in sea-wrinkles,
The distance
(Such a lonesome cowboy)
Only shrugged
And walked away.
How were you to know
What passions
Stood on their toes
For a better look
When you brushed your hair
From your forehead –
They were undone!
The vacant sun
Has better manners
Than anyone.
When you rose

In the first, slender light,
It touched your shoulder –
But only a little –
As if to say,
Excuse me, you dropped this,
Having risen all night to see you.

For Remembering How to Live Without You

Your loneliness and mine
Added together
Make one ingenuous loneliness.

No one will believe this but you.
When you were here it rained each night.
Each morning found you

Beached against me like an irrefutable ark.
Vast, self-conscious island,
You said with eyes closed.

When you left, your pairs
Of slight nocturnal sighs went with you.
I listen to my ears ring now,

The sound of me getting nowhere.
Though I'm telling you there are mountains so distant
It hurts to look.

If there are two kinds of loving,
As everybody thinks he knows,
Two kinds of dying,

Then one of each is easy,
Like the sadness that weds us.
There are two ways to be alone:

One is filled with sunlight
And the yellowing aspen turn it, by alchemy,
Into themselves.

A Discrete Love Poem

This is for you, with your umbrella,
Your suitcase stuffed with roadmaps,
And the fatal blouse unbuttoned.

This is not for your precarious bedroom.

I couldn't help but notice
As several of your possessions assumed false identities:
The clock, for instance,
And your mother's portrait.

I couldn't keep my eyes off that space between your breasts,
A tract of liberated ground.

And later, when the bed sank
Like an earthen raft in the middle of a field, well…

Just the same,
This is for that night your body was neither here nor there.

The Stone's Throw

Tell me something. I don't care what.
Tell me despair is a dress that opens;

The nail, doubtless, is driven straight down
Into the twisted cedar post.

Say death is listening at the door.

Tell me how, between opposites, to tell
The relative from the absolute;

Why the creek sobs out at the start of spring,
Though the spring sun, among stars, is undistinguished.

Paper rose, stone's throw: show me the smallest necessities
Joining to complete the world.

The Longest Distance Between Two Points

You know this already.
I stood without warning and wandered around.

The same air hangs in the house till after the auction.
Who doesn't live before his time?

The trotlines cross from bank to bank:
Pulled downstream like apron strings,
Certain catgut lines with hooks,
Certain trout, yet uncaught.

Inside one, one blue-tail fly
And a drop of fisherman's blood.

Maybe you watch from an attic window
And think of me
As your breath on the glass comes between us.

Maybe you walk through a park, embracing
One tree after another.

Maybe you have the feeling of having been gone a long time.
Now that you're missing, the harvest is this:

Light fails, wind falls back,
The earth is saved in the heart's cellardark.

Lullaby in Praise of Death

You are pretending to adjust the roses;
I pretend I'm sitting down.

Love, everything is a deal.
The grass doesn't mind, the magnolia leaps,

We kill the stars
(And other things) by naming them.

Ideas struggle passionately against thoughts,
The magnolia leaps.

God's old clothes, the northern lights,
Are not explanation enough,

And the instinct to praise is
Sometimes accompanied by a ridiculous dream:

Loneliness surrenders in the olive grove.
Under the glass table,

Under the night sky which resembles the table
Because covered with blossoms,

You were well hidden!
Your green or blue-green dress

Was cut from the unqualified flag
Which falls easily and is never defeated.

Fool's Errand

Alone, like a feather in the air,
An occasional sadness the weather knows
Comes to earth as a bend in the road.

The winter is at its most instructive
As other sadnesses fall
Across the democracy of objects.

Those that aren't shy
Introduce themselves –
Fool's Errand, Clowns of Anguish –

The Equitation of Beautiful Young Girls
Is an exemplary sadness,
As is The Whale's Parasol.

I want to part company
With linear extent,
Congenital heartbreak,

Where the raven goes and snow comes from.
I want distance washed clean,
Unencumbered by facts;

The red cactus flower
To slip into my shirt at dusk
And be the heart's boat.

I want Clowns of Anguish to raise the sail,
And a white handkerchief
Waving from shore.

Lemon Ode

for Neruda

Charmless and strange
At the same time,
The lemon can be opened
To interpretations,
Can encourage dispute,
Ignore abuse, absolve itself
From doubt.
(Never doubt the lemon!)

Solemnity can be forgotten
Like an apricot
Wrapped in newsprint
But not the lemon!
The lemon is always evident,
Elegant, elemental,
Swimming in clarity,
Washed in kitchen-light.

Is the lemon an oboe
On its way to an island
Because you say so?
Only the lemon
Can imagine its own precision,
Though the undecided lemon
Is more precise.

The lemon, audacious,
Drips on the barometer,
Occupies a chair.

The lemon,
As it grows, reaches.

The lemon, reckless,
Thinks, suffers,
Hopes and constantly recites,
Like the cousin
Who reminds you of a saint.

The lemon, as it burns, overflows.
The lemon, which is sour,
Makes demands.

Ode to the Brown Paper Bag

Mystery joins things together.
  – Vallejo

Let's be more specific.
For instance, the brown paper bag.
We must not say the night is black.
Behind the night is what is black.
The bag is candid and opaque.
Consider the women with identical eyebrows,
Humiliated in the market.
Without a brown bag,
Everyone knows their brands of napkin.
And what of husbands if they are sent?
They blush at the check-out girl,
The boys in white aprons.
How can they face the streets home?
But give them a brown paper bag,
Everyone thinks they've bought an ant farm
Or a box of soap.
Mystery joins things together:
Potatoes and oranges,
Lots of oranges,
A few potatoes.
A loaf of bread is friendly as a school bus
When swaddled in brown paper.
Which brings to mind
All the embarrassments
We'll never fit into a small mysterious bag.
And we are diminished for this.

Rosary of Conspiracies

for Stuart

On one hand, the connivance of symmetry, analogy, the heart.
Opposing this, the conspiracy of coincidence, surface,
Ellipsis, the intrigue of mismatched socks.

Is anyone else as confused as I am? It's unlucky
To be in the middle. Even my black suit is oxymoronic.
There's a conspiracy of truth, one of confusion, confederacies

Of process and music. There is watercress
In the millrace, lots of it.
The saw blade's teeth conspire to divide the tree.

The mother, though dead, is wearing her most beautiful dress.
She plans to lie down all the time now.
There's a conspiracy of son and daughters and father.

They go over each other and over the dead
Like a rosary. The mother will not concur
For death is self-devotion.

No wonder the relatives are sad.

How They Go On

The otherwise beautiful girl
With eyes closed
Is not exactly sleeping.

A reverie of dust
obscures the photographs,
Endures the unendurable furniture.

If not to wake her,
If not, softly,
To ask what is left

Under this last, most oceanic circumstance,
The relatives lean in one by one,
As if she might tell them

How it is.
Her ears are more like seashells now,
Where those who loved her

Bend to listen, listen,
And move on,
The same as if they heard and understood.

Another Story

I always thought you favored the bride
Of Arnolfini, though I look nothing like him

And would never wear his hat.
They hold hands, as lovers will,

But hers is turned upward in his
As if he is showing us

That it is empty. Her left hand tells
Another story, resting on her belly

Full with child. They are almost floating
Inside their clothes. They more than float

In the mirror, or between two mirrors.
As is often the case in such matters,

One of the mirrors is really a door
Where a second couple stands, smaller and less clear,

Though similar, asking to be us
For as long as we stay here.

Ode to Significance

Implications arrive in unfamiliar places:
Invading the finespun unbelievable

Down of your arm,
Moving over to accommodate a few trees
(Though each one is

And is dying to tell
An irrelevant version of the river),

Converting them to a noisy green,
A zephyr is not unlikely.
Sweet dreams

Like sailing into wind
No longer seemed equivocal,

And leverage is a property
We aspire to deserve.
If we opened our eyes

That would make two of us, and yet,
Not so –

Inside the knife's edge, the cut
Occupies itself
In study of the obscure.

The truth considers turning back.
I forget who you are,

Since I love you.
But when you say,
It's the wind explains the weathervane,

I think I see what you mean.

Fugue for a Drowned Girl

It is the time of evening that promises miracles to anyone who will believe them. People come out to their porches to see what it's like disappearing. Without regret they move around to the other side. Animals come down to water. The time of evening when trees on the edge of the forest might step into the clearing. Riverstones rub together with a sound like the turning of locks, or like bells, held tightly in both hands.

The wind comes up from the pasture as if looking for someone or thinking of the sea. Shadows of clouds ascend the canyon walls: huge trees growing hundreds of feet and disappearing in smoke. The wind has searched the riverbed down to the coast. It has returned with its arms full of branches.

Each night the sun goes down looking more and more like the moon. Each night the sound of bells moving away. Each night the moon comes up looking more and more like the only way out. Surely no one suspects her weeping. No one suspects her sadness as she thinks of the smallness of the sea, or of cattle returning from pasture. There are rows of glass jars filled with moonlight and the sound of bells approaching.

Without encouragement, without being asked, a little blood has joined the water. Children rush into the schoolyard. Late sunlight fills the high clouds. Surely no one suspects her weeping. The river looks the same. People drink it and bathe in it. They comb it into their hair. Her flesh by now is the color of silt. Her bones might be willow sticks. Fish swim into her hair. One by one the lights in her nails go out.

IMAGINARY TIMBER

IV

Getting a Word In

Very sad,
Having to
Come out of nowhere,

The rain
We've been waiting for
Is waiting too.

Trees,
By now,
Have had enough daylight.

They'd like,
Please,
To sleep it off.

If nothing
Else, nothing
Else.

Behind our backs
Things mean themselves.
Violins crack

From wanting to exist.
It's hard, getting a word in.
I'm waiting

To arrive inside my clothes,
If nothing else,
Willing

To be (having to
Come out of nowhere)
Very sad.

To a Friend I Can't Find

What about this, after all.
How does it follow?
I rent a converted garage
With shower curtains on a pipe
To divide the room in two.
I have a photograph of you
Like a grave
That I look into.
When we still lived in Colorado,
Sometimes you were happy
Without meaning it.
My sister is still in love with you.
I live in the South. I do a job. It rains.
When I let myself down,
It's easy,
And no one's left out.
The old landlord is a real goner;
I think he crossed over
And forgot to die.
He smells like piss and comes to say good-bye
Each afternoon before his nap,
And again at night.
Death can be embarrassing
When it's less than fatal.
This morning when he came over
Asking for a shave,
A starling hung from the window screen,
Like a convict on the fence,
And looked in.
Its feathers were covered with ice.
I soaped the old man's jaw

And the chainlink creases in his neck,
And I cut him once, a little.
He was alive one more time and trying
For the hang of it.
I know he'll die without meaning it.
At dusk the starlings swarm in
Like rivers of starvation.
Their dry-axle noise
Flows past the open door and eddies
In a few trees. They mean something.
They follow. They set each other off
Like fire in a good wind.
Well enough
Is never left alone;
My sister still loves you.
And you must know this, too:
After the flood
The living started digging out.

Rainshadow

If only we could agree that the worst isn't bad,
That only the means remain of the end,
Then the ghost we give up, the believable,

Would long have outlived its usefulness.
My disintegrating father likes to imagine
The family dead live on

In the branches of a sugar pine
On the mesa, by the springhouse.
His naming the improbable invites the impossible.

My father lives in rainshadow.
He keeps a porcelain cup in a branch, like a nest,
To taste the springwater when it's coldest;

Such reasonable furniture becomes us.
If the spring is strong in drought,
We take it on faith the tree is why.

When my father, like water, lies down in the shade,
I'll know where to find the empty cup.
I'll open a window and turn on the lights;

It will look like someone is home.

Hermits

The more I see of people, the more I like my dog.
And this would be good country if a man could eat scenery.

The lake's ice gives light back to the air,
Shadows back to water.

In wet years the land breathes out,
And a crop of limber pines jumps into the open
Like green pioneers.
In dry years
Beetles kill them with roadmaps
Under the skin.

The land breathes in.
The sun goes down,
And the whole sky cracks like rivermud in drought.

A few trees make it each time,
As if some tide carried them out, away from the others.

They say a tree that falls in timber
Goes down in good company:
Snow drifts in and it all goes soft.

They say a ghost is a ghost
That doesn't know it's dead yet.

Those limber pines die standing, lightning-struck, wind broke,
And enough good pitch
For a hermit's winter.

The cabin stood; the man was long dead.
Packrats nested in the firewood,
And a crowd of medicine bottles held forth on the shelf.

When hermits die
They close their eyes. They never hear
The parson sermonize how somewhere
There is hope where no hope was.

Tanglefoot,
Dead-On-Your-Feet,
A chance to be alone for a chance to be abandoned,
Everything is lost or given.

Hermits never know they're dead till the roof falls in.

That Falling We Fall

That falling we fall, dying we rise
Are the descant pleasantries of terror.
Circumstance leaves us standing with flowers.

Everything sufficient is invented.
What is said, therefore, must be
Taken to heart and taken back:

Blue whales
Going under, the gesture of their tails
Says *amaryllis*,
Elegantly and too late; beautiful women,
Ugly women, the grace of God,

Joy, no joy; the dead,
Their arms raised like violin bows
About to begin, begin to sway slowly together.

My mother was friendly, they will like her.
They will comfort her.
They will tell her this
Will never happen again,

This will never happen again.

Three Songs of the One-Man Band

Because they long for bodies, three saints
Run wind-sprints through a city which exists. It is raining.
They race over umbrellas
Like the sound of three bells.
The unhoped-for (keep this in mind)
Is upon us.
The saint with fists made of roses
Calmly aspires, wins every time.

*

Because they will die surrounded by water,
Venetian children wear three kinds of embroidered stockings.
Their shoes are made to float or be filled with flowers.
They chase after the beggar, the one-man band;
Their mothers stand on corners holding bouquets.

*

Because friends, by turns, are saying good night,
The sentimental boatman weeps openly –
Three handkerchiefs full of tears –
And no one will sit on his lap.
The drowning boat has something to tell us.
It is not joking.
Its reflection, indivisible,
Conforms to a vagrant wave.

Consideration of the Sphere

Suppose for a moment you emerge on the frontier of laughter.
Every laugh, silly or cruel, stands like timber,
Branches impatient for a squall.

Assess the importance of this fragrance, obscure,
Unforgettable, unplaceable:
Not quite the halter left on a mule,
Hobbled in the rain.

Examine a certain shrub, laden with pods,
Each a miniature coffin.
Allow for each seed, a lace fan, falling coyly down.

Think of the way you whistle
As you pour kerosene on your shadow;
How it leaps up, bright in the afternoon.

Remember the story of the Inca king
Who covered his body with gold dust before dawn,
Rowed to the lake's sacred center.
As the sun struck him he dove
And rose up what he was.

Consider what is in us
Without us.

Widow Osborne

The widow pulled the shades one day
And that was it. The world slipped
Her mind, the house
Slipped its moorings and drifted out.
Shall we say the widow
Knows better than to go away?

Her house is poormouthed, daunted,
Clapboard-curled and trying to remember
The last flecks, like sparks, of yellow paint.
The foundation is dry masonry
Of stones annoyed with their neighbors.
Just the place

For a widow that likes to scare boys
Who fish below her house at night
Where the creek rolls down through uncut hay
Like widowsleep,
And steal the icicles from her porch in winter.
The house buckled in till the eaves touched the ground,

A child's clumsy hands
Collapsing on a moth.
All you can see from the county road
(You'd never know she was alive)
Is the big tin roof,
Like a window in the green side-hill.

On the other side of the world,
Crickets fish for sadness in chokedamp air,
And the sun eases into its weary admission

That things are better here,
Green fire in the tallest pines,
The widow in her bath.

Navigation

Evergreens have reasons
For stopping where they do,
At timberline or the clean edge
Of sage and prairie grass.
There are quantities of wind
They know they cannot cross.

They come down from the tundra
On waves of ridges and stop,
Staring out over open country,
Like pilgrims on the shore
Of an unexpected ocean.
The sky is still the sky, they know;
It won't understand ordinary language.

Meet my mother, twice removed,
Who could tell the time from stars.
She said everything is its own reward,
Grief, poverty, the last word.
Evening was her favorite time
And she walked along the shore of trees,
Carrying herself as if afraid
She might give herself away.
She called this being quiet.

Just inside the treeline, out of the wind,
Father built a handrail along the path.
She'd stand there like a sailor's wife
And stare at the high plains as dark came on.
She said mountains might be islands
But the sky is still the sky.

She'd wait for the ranch lights
On the prairie to come out
Like a fallen constellation.
She said waiting is its own reward,
The lights are only reasons.

Cache la Poudre

The whole world
(Which you said I was
To you)
Thought it might lie down a minute
To think about its rivers.
It puts the case to you,
Admitting nothing,
The way rapids speculate
On the topic of stones.

The farmers on the Poudre should have known
From snuff-tin rings worn into their pockets:
Matter is a river
That flows through objects;
The world is a current
For carrying death away.
Their wooden fenceposts rotted fast in the bog
So they quarried stone posts from nearby bluffs.
You can guess what they looked like;

The worst of it was
They meant it.
Rivers neither marry,
Nor are they given in marriage;
The body floats
Face down in the soul;
The world turns over.

Those gritstone fences sank out of sight
Like a snowshoe thrown in the river.
The whole world

(Of human probability)
Lay under that hawk we found,
Face down, wings spread,
Not so much
Flying into it,
As seizing its double in the snow.

GOD'S MISTRESS

1984

GOD'S MISTRESS

Salt

Hematite Lake

There is another kind of sleep,
We are talking in it now.
As children we walked in it, a mile to school,
And dreamed we dreamed we dreamed.

By way of analogy, consider nightfall.
In relation to the light we have, consider it final –
Still falling from the night before
With ourselves inside it like ore in the igneous dark.

So I went for a walk around Hematite Lake
To watch the small deer they call fallow deer
Dreamed to life by sleeping fields.
Someone had taken the water,

Don't ask me who. The wild swans were
Still there, being beautiful,
And the geese lay down in the grass to sleep.
The shallows, now dry, were peopled with lilies:

Their poor, enormous heads reeled in the aquatic air.
The path was drifted in with gossamer
From the tree-spiders' nightly descent:
A monumental feather the geese flew over.

What happens is nothing happens.
What happens is we fall so far
Into a sleep so manifold,
Not even nightfall, whose gold we are, can find us.

Watershed

Here the land is tilted
Like a gambrel roof. The world
Slopes away from the Great Divide,
And all the people
And all the trees
Lean in the same direction
Just to stand up straight.

Even lies that lean that way are true,
Like wilsome pines at timberline.
When I die and turn to rain,
I'd like to fall into the distance
And stay awhile.

I'd be happy to be smaller,
Where close at hand is out of reach
And everything nearby is blue:
The denim work-clothes of the men,
Their axes in the spruce,
The spruce, the sky,
The knife that cuts the rain in two, the lie.

Fragments Written While Traveling
Through a Midwestern Heat Wave

1.

However lonely we were before
Becomes unclear
In our next loneliness.
All summer long the rain
Stayed west of the mountains.

2.

Underneath this landscape of sighs
Is a landscape of feathers,
One of blood, and yes,
A landscape of earth and trees and sky.
The soil of Oklahoma
Is leaving again.
Heaven is west of where it falls.

3.

Down here in the level world
Oil rigs make love
To the earth beneath the wheat.
All afternoon the wind blows hot.
The river is a piece of dirty string.
Like huge somnambulating farmers,
Dust-devils work the fallow ground.

4.

The real farmers
Disc their fields on tractors
With hopeful, yellow umbrellas
And raise white flags of surrender
Which keep the flying ants
From swarming near their faces.

5.

I'll tell you what the soul is made of:
More dust.
Behind each harrow
In each field
A plume takes to the wind.
The farmers,
At last,
Are freeing themselves
By setting free the soil.

Drift Fence

Whose hungry souls are these,
all in a row,
already lost...

and are they penitent
in shackles of barbed wire
on the bare hillside?

Whatever they were before –
that is to say,
whatever living pine trees are –

these twist and suffer.
The drift fence
drops off the hill

and shambles down through timber
without separating
anything.

It affirms the imaginary
line by wandering.
It reels from tree to tree,

lost in sundry
mystifications
until the forest yields

to pasture
and the landscape
opens its eye.

They cross the open country,
single file,
faithful,

each bearing
an undivided sorrow
back into the world.

Old Men on the Courthouse Lawn, Murray, Kentucky

You might call this
The far side of the river
If you ever lived in Indiana,
Ohio, Illinois.

There is no city
On the river's far side,
Just middling towns as similar
As printed roses on a widow's dress –

Perhaps you knew her.
She never moved away.

Nor are the old men
On the courthouse lawns in any of these towns
Any less like flowers
Since they rise at first light

And dress alike in overalls,
Gray shirts and caps,
As if they still had something
To do.

They have less to do
Than flowers.

They gather at the courthouse
From first light to last.
They chew their Mammoth Cave,
Their Copenhagen.

They comment on the height of the river.
They're too far gone to give a damn

About women anymore.
Tobacco stains bloom on the walk.

And now these men seem more to me
Like harmless old bees
Gathering the sweetness of the last, thin light
On the only side of the river they know.

High Plains Rag

But like remorse
the prairie grass
seeks emptiness,

increases
in its sleep,
gets even

with the fragrant,
stoic sage.
Oh, it is witless

and blind.
It cannot remember
what it was doing

with all that wind.
It waits
for a thimbleful of rain.

It populates such distances
it must be brave
but prairie grass

bends down in sorrow
to be so lost,
and like remorse

feels
so nearly endless
it cannot ever stop.

Three Sonnets

Where I live   distance is the primal fact
The world is mostly   far away and small
Drifting along through cause and effect   like sleep
As when the distance   unlikeliest of stems
Bears the unlikely   blossom of the wind
Engendering our only weather   dry
Except in winter   pine trees live on snow
So greedy   pulling down these drifts that bury
The fences snap   the trunks of smaller trees
If the forest wants   to go somewhere it spreads
Like a prophecy   its snow before it
Technology   a distant windy cause
There is no philosophy   of death where I live
Only philosophies   of suffering

Virga

The rain we prayed for
that never came
couldn't
save the pasture now,
so we pray for rain
to keep the woods from burning.

Thick clouds of yellow pollen
rise from the evergreens:
fire of an order more like ours,
that flowers from loneliness.
Desire's object, being beautiful,
measures distance from us.

Contrary to belief
lightning strikes the same place
as often as it wants.
Trees are waiting
to be angels, too.
The air thrums with static

between heaves of thunder.
Bolts poke holes in the timber
like cigarette burns
in a green dress.
We pray against the wind.
In the distance some rain

that falls evaporates
before it reaches the ground:

a brushstroke on the air
that falls without falling, meaning –
the rain prays for us, in a way.
We call it a dry *spell*,

as in *enchantment*.

The Importance of Green

Small towns are for knowing who's poor.
I recognized her, the welder's daughter.
In a store she touched a green dress,
But she couldn't buy it.
The salesgirl scolded, making her ashamed.

That's how the sun comes through the open door today,
Still poor from night rain.
The road to town is a muddy tongue.

The forest stands ajar
And I could get up from this chair and disappear
Into the coldly steaming pine,
Which is like the next great philosophy
That will pity no one.

Its particularity is awesome.
The blue flower whose name I never remember
Joys through the eyeholes of a horse's skull,
A horse named Lola we kids rode.

Past the anthill roofed with mothwings,
Handfuls of elk hair like smoke the barbed wire snagged.
At sunset the invisible lakes rise and color
Like pieces of the biggest mirror ever broken.

Like those things,
But not those things exactly.
Interchangeable, let's say.

I could walk through groves where there are no paths
Until I was shrouded in cobwebs – I've done it before –
Like someone who lived in a dark cellar forever.
Like someone who lived in a dark cellar forever,

Needles resilient under my feet,
I could walk out into the sunlight
And tell you the truth:

The girl who wanted the dress doesn't matter –
No more than the dress itself,
Or green.

For Our Better Graces

God loves
the rain, not us.
Ours is
what spills over,
what we look for
that finds us:
innocence
by association.
Cloud shadows
feel their way,
rapid and blind,
over the face
of the prairie.
Pine trees
atop the ridge
row the world
into the dampblack sky.
God's mistress
rides by
on a feather of water.
After she is gone
her fragrance
is everywhere.

Water Table

How shy the attraction
of simple rain to east wind
on the dry east side
of the Neversummer Mountains.
Each afternoon clouds sidle in
just so, but rain is seldom.
Here what they call the water table
is more like a shooting star.
Streams that surface in the spring
are veins of fool's gold.
The water we count on
is run-off from high snows
gone underground.
The rest, the rain,
is a tinker's damn.

*

My mother is favored
in being buried here, where she was born.
My father is from the East.
He tried to understand these hills
by building miles of roads and fences,
looking for water in unlikely places.
When we had enough fence
he kept building roads –
up canyons, through timber,
with axe and bar.
Sometimes he found old mining roads
unused in years.
Such innocence terrifies stones.

*

Midyear,
if you drive on the pasture,
the grass won't spring back anymore,
so come September we saw the tracks
of everywhere he'd been since then.
To the rain it would have looked like a child's first attempt
to write his name.

Once he found an infant's grave
near a failed claim.
The writing on the stone
was also like a child's hand,
written by someone
who didn't know anything
about writing in stone.
It didn't say a name, it said,
She never knew a stranger.

*

Before the snow one September,
a man who lived here years ago
came to pay a visit.
He wore a white shirt,
sleeves rolled to the elbows,
and trousers the color of autumn grass.
He wouldn't come inside
or lean across the fence
the way a neighbor will.
He didn't care to stay,
although he'd lived here thirty years

and made this place from nothing
with his hands.

He showed my father a hidden spring
with fool's gold in the water.
He showed me how to use a witching-wand.
He said he mined for thirty years
and never found a thing worth keeping,
said the time to sink a well
is a dry year, in the fall.
The next we heard he'd died
somewhere west of here.
Then I had this dream:

*

In the driest month of a dry year
my father took it in his mind
to dig out fallow springs
all across the mountains.
He had roads to all of them.
He thought someone might be thirsty.
I asked how people stayed alive
before he came here
from the East.
He guessed they must have died.

*

I could say I understand
what goes on underground:
why all old men are miners
and children turn to gold-flecked water;
I could explain the weather,
like when the wind comes out of the east

and meets the simple rain.
The wind is strong.

The rain has slender shoulders.
The rain can't say
what it really means
in the presence of children
or strangers.

GOD'S MISTRESS

The Spruce Forest

Misericord

Out at the end of a high promontory
above the dim, oceanic prairie,
we built a little fire for warmth.

Who ever doubted that the earth fell from the sky?
As though it had traveled a great distance to reach us

and still could not reach us,

though we held our hands out to it,
some vague intention, some apprehension
occurred between us.

That night we slept in the snow
by a half-frozen lake.
I could smell the woodsmoke in your hair.

We heard the earth cloud over, clear again,
the low voltage of granite and ice,
and everlastingness

let fall the moment
like a girl slipping out of her silk chemise.

But forget all that.
I wanted to tell you, the girl,
that when I woke in the morning

small frogs were singing from the lake as if
we had become transparent in our sleep.

A Second Time

It was the year I cut logs for the new house and roads, roads like veins that let the timber bleed. You wore a different shawl each day. It was the year I shot the white mare, and her filly, equally white, refused to follow the herd to winter pasture. It was the year you left me the first time, before the aspen turned. Then it was the winter the sky couldn't get off the ground. East wind went down the chimney and filled the house with smoke.

The new house consisted of sticks and strings and numbers on scraps of paper. Facts are mercenary bastards. Spring was the fallacy that brought you back, but nothing in the world could hold you. The last storm we hauled feed to the snowbound horses. The white filly stood her ground apart. You fed that rowdy gang instead, those bluejays, vainglorious thieves that loitered in the pines behind the house. I wouldn't say you tamed them, but they flew down to you for crumbs.

It took all June to haul foundation stone from the mountain, to screen enough sand from the river for mortar. It was the year we cut hay between squalls, and the aspen turned early, their self-elegy, and the evergreens I'd cut turned into walls. You scolded the aspen outside your window for staying green when all the rest were gold. Now that you're gone a second time I already know what it's like. It snows inside. Jays swirl around the house like a blue shawl. Loud and bright they follow me whenever I go out – to the barn, the spring, even into the patient woods.

It's been storming for a week. The quakies are bare except for the one by the window, which is gold, in snow, and won't let go its leaves. The evergreens are singed with frost so that each is delineated, individual, each in its own doorway of ice. The new roof is half-finished. It snows inside. The early settlers here made houses out of trees and tried to live. When they starved out and moved on, they burned their houses down to get the nails back.

Explication of an Imaginary Text

Salt is pity, brooms are fury,
The waterclock stands for primordial harmony.

The spruce forest, which is said to be
Like a cathedral
Indicates proliferation of desire.

The real meaning of the beginning
Will not become clear until later, if ever.

Things no longer being what they were,
Artifice poses as process,
The voice is tinged with melancholy.

The teacup, the brass knuckles, and the pearl-handled razor
Resist interpretation

As if to say
That half the wind is in the mind
And half in the mind of the wind.

Speaking through the character
Who comes to faith on his deathbed,

The author makes apology
For saying things he didn't mean.
Little girl-cousins with ribbons in their hair

Confuse him with their names and are carried away
By laughter. Thus,

The force of love comes from belief,
Hate is from lack of doubt.
Paradox by paradox the narrative proceeds

Until half the stars are *absolute tears.*
The other half are *mirrors.*

Dark Angel

To the things we call opaque, the sun,
which has no shadow,
gives new shadows every day.

People fall
into this category.
Other kinds of shadows

are less popular,
like dry weather.
When an ocean goes away

the prairie is just its shadow staying.
Even the wind
makes shadows sometimes –

that's what snowdrifts are,
and why they can't lie down except
in the small lees

of draws and clumps of sage,
and why, up higher,
the deep timber fills.

Mountains ring these tides and swells
of sage and grass.
When the sun goes down

the mountains cast their shadows,
ardent nets, though sad,
over the shadow of water,

clear to the other side,
but not to be drawn
back in.

Rendezvous

During that time
There were times –
You may not believe it –
You, abandoned, and I,
A lonely man,
Would meet.
We took the result
For a more exact definition,
Which is to say,
Our bodies were too much for us.

I would give you a rose,
You would leave without your shoes.
It would seem to me,
Looking back,
Necessity wasn't so bad.
I gave you a rose, you left your shoes,
Still, there was more attrition
Than you think:
You forgot to tell me
What I never thought to ask;
I would wait
With passionate indifference,
You would not arrive.

Weather was mannered then,
In its uncertainty.
The well's ice went all the way down
Like a nail.
The line implied
By line of sight

Was a delirious streamer
Fixed to us.
We were also something like a nail,
One that fixed
A significant location,
Though not in itself
Significant.

To See the Stars in Daylight

You have to go down
in a deep mineshaft or a well,

down where you can imagine the incomparable
piety of the schoolbus,
the wherewithal of bees,

down where you can be a drawer full of dust
as night comes on under full sail,

and the smooth rain,
in its beautiful armor,
stands by forever.

I believe
there's a fiddle in the wings

whose music is full of holes
and principles beyond reason.
It binds our baleful human hearts

to wristwatches and planets,
it breaks into fragments which are not random.

The girl in the white dress kneels by the riverbank
and, like the willow, leans
and trails her fingers in the current.

She doesn't know about the damselfly, exquisitely blue,
that has fallen asleep on her pillow.

Girl on the Pier

The pier is less like a bridge than a well,
Since it leads to water.

Bridges are for crossing in pairs.
Standing alone at the end of the pier

The girl is brave and fragile, more beautiful
At this moment than anything in the world.

Her salty handkerchief wants to be a sail.
The ship is long since out of sight;

The distance where she looks for it
Whiles away in blue.

How I would like to hold her,
To bring her back from the end of the pier!

Analogy breaks down when it comes to tears.
When it comes to oceans bridges don't prevail.

The girl thinks the pier is a bridge that fails.
The waves, she thinks, must be ideal

Since they break behind her on the actual shore:
That's the genius of the pier.

The girl looks down at her handkerchief
To find a single eyelash

Whereby she makes a sentimental wish,
A wish that water seeks to fulfill,

Whether salt or fresh,
In the wave or the well.

Practice

The world arrived
so carefully packed
in time,
in time to open,
it could have been
God's parachute.
We booby-trapped it.
God, you will remember
from the Old Testament,
was a terrorist.
Now He's a generalization.
We've taken to scaring ourselves.
We scare the ozone layer.
But today, still spinning
around the world's axis,
which is imaginary,
I was permitted to walk home
again through writhing spring.
Leafy things and flowers
in earnest everywhere,
ignoring fear.
If it was anything

it was a garden.
Then, by the gymnasium
I saw a girl
in a green leotard with long sleeves.
She wasn't just any girl,
she was a dancer,
which is to say only
she didn't regret

her body.
She moved in it
and it moved.
She spun herself around.
She wasn't dancing, exactly,
more like she was practicing a dance,
getting the moves right,
which moved me
even more.

Sure I wanted her,
but I stood quietly
as she practiced dancing
alone, without music,
and then I continued on.
It wouldn't have been a good thing
to interrupt that solitude,
identical with her body,
or risk frightening her
with speech.

Scrimshaw

There you are,
end of sorrow,
so abstract
in your black dress,

so effortlessly
formal.

You trail your left hand
down the banister
and avoid the light
from the chandelier.

How like an actual
girl you are,
drawing near,

how your bearing
requires
the scrimshaw fan you carry.

When you open it
to conceal a hint
of color on your cheek,
it reveals

the arctic distances
of bone,

and sailors setting out
in tiny hopeful ships.

Leaving the Tilted City

Love, if you exist
don't tell anyone.

Murderers line the streets like glass doors,
and merciful lies aren't wrong.

We'll tell them I'm the inspector of lightning
or a failed puppeteer.

They won't know the difference
if we leave the tilted city,

if we float downriver
on a raft of mandolins.

I remember believing in you.
I believed you were there to answer.

But that was before
I had ever touched you.

Sempiternal

Out at sea the sun
was shining,
but only in one place,
like a silver dish
on the rain-darkened water.
A single whale,
sated with love,
steaming north from Baja,
was too distant to see,
but we could

see where he was breathing:
a tree made of water
and filled with silver light
appeared on the air,
already falling,
and after a whale-breath,
reappeared –
the selfsame form –
a little farther
north each time.

After the Papago

for Ruth Underhill

I've done it now.
I've come back where something good is my desire.
And now, though at first I didn't know,
It has happened.

I like it and gather it up.

I crawled off and I couldn't stand it.
I thought of my house and I went there.
When I saw my house I couldn't stand it.
I turned around and talked to myself.
I remembered you.

The water runs quickly.
The water plants grow.

I like it and gather it up.

Small trout are swept backward downstream.

There is my wind and it reaches me.
So very nicely and wetly it blows.

There is my cloud and it reaches me
So very nicely and wetly.

I like it and gather it up.

Now I turn homeward
On the homeward road.

GOD'S MISTRESS

Half the Stars

A Poem from the Edge of America

There are ways of finding things, like stumbling on them.
Or knowing what you're looking for.
A miss is as good as a mile.
There are ways to put the mind at ease, like dying,
But first you have to find a place to lie down.

Once, in another life, I was a boy in Wyoming.
I called freedom home.
I had walked a long time into a high valley.
A river cut through it. It was late,
And I was looking for a place to lie down,

Which didn't keep me from stumbling
On something, believe me, I never wanted to find.
It was only the skeleton of someone's horse,
Saddled and bridled and tied to a tree.
When I woke in the morning it was next to me.

The rider must have wandered off, got turned around
And lost. It must have been winter.
The horse starved by the tree.
When we say, *what a shame*, whose shame do we mean?
In earnest of stability water often rages,

But rivers find their banks again, in earnest of the sea.
This ocean I live on can't hold still.
I want to go home to Wyoming and lie down
Like that river I remember with a valley to flow in,
The ocean half a continent away.

The horse I spoke of isn't a reason,
Although it might be why.

Above Half Moon

Not even a bird can sleep in thin air, a thousand feet higher than the highest trees on Half Moon Pass, where summer lasts a month or less, and the rest is just high wind and low clouds, like now, a landscape removed to the sky. Even the snow can't stand it here, it jumps at the first breeze and feathers down to the timber.

A single drift, a crescent, naps in the lee of the cabin. Whoever built this claim a hundred years ago must have been a lunatic, or driven. He chipped out his mineshaft, one man's monument to hard luck, an obelisk of air pointing straight down. Maybe he counted on Holy Cross Mountain for grace. Maybe he just liked being alone in the sky.

The logs still show where his adze bit in. He fitted them with broad axe and bucksaw, and pegged them together the way they used to make the hulls of ships, but this was built with wind in mind and too much empty sky around. The walls are double, pinestraw in between: a house inside a house with double-shuttered windows, a flower made of timber, whose trail down is a crooked stem.

How he hauled his timber up the talus slope, a mile of switchbacks, was, I'd guess, a mule. He hauled the logs a log at a time. Who knows how he got that woodstove home, or what he thought of moonless nights awash in stars, or if the kerosene light seemed cold and far away. He must have hauled his firewood too, and melted snow sometimes for water.

I guess there was no place to go from here. The door opens on a view of the mountain when the weather is clear or the clouds are down below. The lake below the mountain is called The Bowl of Tears. I don't know, maybe he was crazy and wanted to be rich. Maybe he wanted to be alone with God. You can see where he nailed tin cans hammered flat and old boot soles over the cracks in the door.

Anthropology

Remember the night you got drunk
and shot the roses?
You were a perfect stranger, Father,
even my bad sister cried.

Some other gravity,
not death or luck,
drew fish out of the sea
and started them panting.

The fish became a man.
The archer's bow became a violin.
I remember the night you searched the sofa
for change

and wept on the telephone.
Some other gravity,
not time or entropy,
pulled the knife down for centuries.

The archers dropped their bows,
harmless as pine needles in the snow.
The knife became a plow
and entered the earth, Father.

Later it became a boat
and some other things –
It isn't a dream but it takes a long time,
for the archer's bow to become a violin.

Upland Birds

I dreamed a tall spruce grove
planted in deep earth.
The branches were full of secret birds
that sang together as well as separately.

When I was young
we hunted wood grouse in deep spruce groves.
We called them fool hens.
We killed them with rocks.

They couldn't fly away very far.
Sometimes they were so confused
they walked right up to us
or perched in easy range and watched.

The kind of grouse we found on the prairie
was a different story.
Living far from trees had made them wary.
They watched the ground for shadows of wings.

They watched the horizon for coyotes and men.
In winter I could find them
among the shacks of an abandoned ranch
that was like a shipwreck on the plains.

It was the only windbreak
for miles of open space.
They'd wait until I was barely close
before they exploded into the sky and drifted

a quarter-mile or so downwind.
And I ran after them.
Each time they'd fly, not far,
before I came too near,

and I ran after them again and again,
until I was too tired to follow anymore,
and miles from home or any tree,
under the blue, enormous sky.

Above timberline we tried to catch ptarmigan.
In summer they are the color of the rocks
and tundra grass they lie down among.
In winter they are white

and lie down in the snow.
We hardly ever saw them,
but when we did we caught them in our hands
and let them go.

On Sharing What We Never Had

Ray, my neighbor, was born in a claim shack that didn't belong to anyone, but Ray owned the whole mountain if owning means you don't have to share. He was twelve years old before he saw a stranger: a peg-legged fisherman working the ponds on Nigger Bob Creek. Ray sneaked up behind a tree and watched till dark.

On the county road the tourists stop to marvel at a large balsam tree, an impossible tire girdling its trunk. That tire went flat in 1940, when Ray and Margie had just been married. Margie said it was a hell of a note. Ray threw the tire over a sapling, not thinking how someday, now, it would fit snug as a ring.

As I drive up to the house, Margie is hanging glass bottles of sugar-water under the eaves. Hummingbirds lace the air around her like a gust of leaves. They perch on her outstretched fingers like jewelry.

Ray and I take fly rods and a fifth of rye up Nigger Bob Creek. They've sold this ground to developers, the ponds are mostly silted-in. We weren't fishing anyway. Why should it hurt to share what we never had a right to? On the way home Ray stops the truck by the balsam tree. He says he still can't figure out why he did that, why a man would do such a thing. He eases the truck back into the road and asks did I ever wonder who Nigger Bob was.

Sara

Sara stays at home.
Her looks are plain.
She paints somber landscapes with sleeping horses.
She hears voices.

She's going to stop living later this afternoon.

Now she's painting the uncut hay waiting in the meadow,
that her father and brothers used to mow
when they were alive.

Sara knows from observation
how it is with trees – without a forest
they can't go on.
Her mother tells Sara not to paint so sad.

Look, she says, standing at the bay window,
cleaning the glass with a white cloth,

It's beautiful, not sad!
The walls of the house are covered with Sara's landscapes.
It's like not having any walls.

The sun is hot on the brim of her straw hat,
and the valley can't imagine itself
without her.
She paints the hay barn, leaning a little,

the snowfence, also leaning,
the pines behind the house and barn

a sadder green than pine trees are.

The house, from the outside, is plain.
Sara paints her mother standing at the window,

a white cloth against the glass.

Whistle

This morning I hoofed out. It was cold as two sticks.
There should be snow by now.
The ground has had enough. It's anvil-hard.
It won't be accepting any more death till spring.

Among patches of red earth abraded by wind
Weedstalks and grass stems and crystalline leaves
Wait to lower themselves back down.
I walked home without leaving tracks, like an angel.

Burnt-out, winterbare, this handbasket
Needs a covering of snow. There should be snow by now.
Earth revealed like this demands a dignity
That was never in us. White veil, black veil,

The bride's, the widow's countenance,
The faces of the dead-by-violent-causes,
It's bad to gaze upon them.
A lace of snow is needed here, permission

To forget.
The creek below the spring whistles under its breath,
Just making believe.

Almost Noon

The water, you remember,
Was so cold it took our breath
Until we laughed. The sun didn't shine down there at all
Except at noon. You remember. No one
Ever took your picture there, but this one:
Granite walls, deep water, cedar, your favorite spot,
Where I threw your ashes into the falls.

I like the hat you're wearing. Father's straw one,
Though it casts your eyes in shadow.
I can tell what time it is
By how much of you is missing.
The children can go swimming now.

Sometimes things happen this way,
And I can't talk about it.
There are smaller, darker shadows gathered in your ears.
They are planning an invasion. Listen,
You can't even hear them.
You are turning to the camera, saying yes.

Still Here

The light is trying trying to be tangible
When it strikes the angle
Of a good blade on the wheel.
Some high silky clouds tune up
For a real Western sunset.
The shadows of things would be alarming
If you didn't know
They were only shadows.
The horses drift in from pasture
With their heads down.
Since horses don't pray they must be grazing.
Lost in tenderness,
They could be, already, in another life.
Ray drives up so slowly,
An old man in a red pickup,
He hardly raises any dust.
He likes leaving things the way they are.
The surface of the earth, let's face it,
Is abrasive.
Things get smaller
Even when they grow.
We sit out back on the cooler, facing west,
With a jug between us.
Ray lifts a tumbler half-full of rum.
Right now I'm a millionaire,
He says and tips it back.
The horses drift off, out of sight
Behind some hills,
The world surrenders its details,
But we're still here,
Riding the edge of failing light –
Steel-dust in a swirl.

Snowherd

The industry of flowers
Is dying young.
My friend Ray, I'm afraid, is gone.
His crook was a shovel,
His flock was water.
Winter his flock was snow,
So Ray built snowfences along the ditches
And shoveled in spring
To make them run.
Ray was a water engineer,
Which means
He filled the reservoir
For the ranchers
On the prairie.

Upwind, downstream,
Almost just in time,
Ray just wanted to help someone
By building a bridge
Across a ditch
Or clearing a neighbor's winter road.
(He even gathered mountain phlox,
Which looks like melting snow,
For a certain widow's windowbox.)
It's hard to be happy
In such a dry country.
Ray filled the reservoir
For the ranches on the prairie,
Where otherwise only weeds would grow.

Up the mountain, early spring,
He shouldered his shovel
Like a single, useless wing.
Under the grass was the last thing he wanted,
Which means he wanted it at last.
All the ditches filled with snow,
The headgates froze.
Moth wings drifted
On windowsills,
And the ants came along in single file.
Each one shouldered a wing
And climbed the window into the sky,
As if to show us humility,
The science of living on.

Shadow-Casting

This boy's father dies.
                              Fine.
                    It always happens.
                                        The boy knows
what to do.
                    He goes fishing the same stretch of water he angled
with his father all his life till now.
                                        The beaver ponds shine
like a string of pearls.
                    It isn't easy to fly-cast a mirror-
finish.
          The ponds are silting in.
                              It always happens.
                                             They turn
into meadows.
                    The stream is choked with sweet-smelling grasses,
cottonwoods, and willows.
                              He knows what to do with fifty feet
of line out, shadow-casting.
                              The loops flash over his head, electric
in the sunlight, as if to illustrate grief, or the hem of a luminous
dress in motion.
                    Then the tapered line rifles out, and the lead-
wing touches water with no more force than its own tiny weight.

The surface breaks.
                    They call them rainbows for a reason.
                                                  The boy
opens his father's clasp-knife to open the fish.
                                        As he does this
some lint trapped under the blade, like a cottonwood seed from

his father's pocket, falls out and parachutes down to the grass, and suddenly this boy, it always happens, doesn't know what to do anymore.

They Haven't Heard the West Is Over

So that no one should forget, and no one be forgotten – isn't that what graves are for? The road from Tie Siding labors up the ridge like an old man in deep snow, leading the ditch like a mule, like always, making the woods by dark. The timber goes from green to blue on its way to the bone-white Divide.

Off the road there, in the lee of the rise (so that no one should forget), in a mixed patch of evergreen and aspen (so that no one be forgotten), you can barely see the rail fence, a brief enclosure, through the living trees.

Rough stones pried from the ground nearby, these markers bear no names. But I know who is buried here, and who repairs the rails. These folk were pioneers, and are, apart from other people: Ap Worster and his wife so frail he could place his hands wholly around her waist.

She wasn't strong enough to live so far away. Ap climbed a haystack when she died. He lay on his back and cried three days. That was 1910. Someone's girl died in winter, before she had a name. They kept her till the ground thawed. Death had done its work by then, and more.

There are others here that I could name and tell about, but the differences between them now are slight: a balsam tree is growing out of someone, someone is covered by an aspen bough, newly fallen.

Besides, these are not like graves in town that no one should forget. These were meant to be forgotten. Some people never stop wanting to disappear into the mountains. Right now the whole of Wyoming opens its rusty arms to the north, and the road from here keeps going, as if it were going somewhere.

Little Anthem

Cool in brindled shade below the springbox,
Willows muster and fold over
In green vaults
To assemble and reassemble the place
My mother planted watercress
A long time, now, ago.

That deep in green was hers,
Safe from deer and safe from horses.

Shallow water doctors the light,
And the vague silt settles down
Vegetable and feathery
Like the inside of a living eye.
The watercress is a secret floating country,
Its own green flag,

With history.
It's quiet here,

Despite the water's
Small gasps of surprise,
But the noise Ernie raised
Repairing the springbox lid
Was an old man's pissing and moaning
And a glorious hurling about of tools in rage.

Father gave orders to stay clear of Ernie,
Whose meanness came from dying slowly,

But my mother sent me down for watercress.
Above my head, a cat's-paw hit the tree.
I knelt and touched the atmosphere
Those numb leaves lived in.
Keeping myself small, I tore up handfuls.
Howling, Ernie sent his hammer arcing.

One of his eyes was made of glass
And it wavered toward me.

What desire
Held me there against which fears?
When my bowl greenly overflowed, I stayed.
When his fury lost its way in sadness, I stayed.
When he set to work again,
I stayed.

And what I stole from him
Was mine.

The Last Man's Club

My grandfather was always sad. Sadly, as a boy, he paddled his canoe along the beautiful Hudson River, which was only then beginning to die. During the first war he was very sad in France because he knew he was having the time of his life. When it was over everyone in America felt like a hero – imagine.

Once a year on Armistice Day, he met with all his friends from the war. They got drunk and recounted the stories of the time when they had thought they were men and the world had seemed entirely possible. They placed empty chairs for certain of the dead, and in the center of the table, a bottle of cognac from France, for the last man of them to drink alone, in honor of the others.

Year after year they gathered to watch each other and themselves disappear, turn into empty chairs. Sooner or later they all were sad. Some of them must have realized they didn't need to join a club for this.

Finally it came down to my grandfather and a man named Oscar Cooper. Neither of them wanted to outlive anyone. They couldn't remember what honor was. When they drank the cognac it didn't taste like anything. They threw the bottle in the river as if they thought it meant that neither of them was alive anymore.

When Cooper died the following year, my grandfather took his rifle out into the yard and fired three shots at the sky. Then he went down to the river and drank himself to sleep. After that he was never sad, not even when the river died.

What Holds Them Apart

In those days they worked from loose stacks to the stationary
baler and tied the bales by hand.

                         Lyle's name means *the island*,
but he doesn't know that.

                  His hayfield, a peat bog, is the
only level ground on this side of the mountain.

                             For a time
I was young enough to catch tadpoles in ditches and take them
home in mayonnaise jars while all the men were haying.

                                   Long
afternoons I fished in the creek that runs through Lyle's
meadow.

      I knew that water down to the bottom stones.

                                   Deep
pools were friends.

                  Fingery willows that snagged my hand-
tied flies were enemies.

                  Lyle never liked the sound of his
name.

      He prefers to work alone.

                        He used to have a family,
but they're gone.

                  When he isn't haying he's building things
by hand.

      He makes tools to make tools to make things like
hay barns and violins and muzzle-loading guns whose barrels
he taps, whose triggers, locks, and hammers he forges.

                                  That
summer he was building a new room on our house.

                               He wanted
me to build retaining walls, so he took me down and showed

me something about the creek I didn't know.

                                                         We shoveled sand
all afternoon.

                 You might think cement is what holds the
stones in a wall together.

                           Masons know it's what holds them
apart.

      And mortar is mostly sand from the river.

                                        I couldn't
see why we needed retaining walls – just because there's
no level ground on this side, and you have to notch the
slope to build on.

                    I couldn't imagine the mountain as a
slower kind of river.

                      We pried big stones from a knoll
of frost-cracked granite.

                       They were angular, irregular.

You could see the whole Medicine Bow and Laramie Peak from
there.

      We loaded the truck bed till the springs were flat,
and then some.

                    I learned to stagger the seams and fit the
random stones by trying different combinations, as if the
wall were a puzzle with one ideal order that doesn't make
a picture, and whose puzzle-parts weigh fifty pounds each,
so it hurts to change your mind.

                              They never really fit
till you tear them down and build them back in order, with
mortar to hold them apart.

                       I remember remembering a photo-
graph I'd seen of the house Lyle was born in.

                                   It was out
on the flats of eastern Colorado.

                 Most of the picture was

pale, cloudless sky.

          There wasn't a tree or a bump on the
land except that house, which was made of the same dirt
and prairie grass it was lost in.

          A house made of earth
that you couldn't see anything from.

          Now Lyle, who doesn't
like the sound of his name, which he doesn't know means
the island, is standing on the roof with a hammer in his
right hand.

          He wears dark glasses and a painter's cap,
an apron full of nails.

          The sun is behind him. I can't
see his face.

I'm hot and tired and I don't understand why we need retaining
walls.

          I shade my eyes and see a red-tailed hawk circling the
deep blue and sun above us.

          I'm trying to say the kind of thing
a man would say.

          I put down this stone and offer,

          That hawk

up there sure has it easy.

          Lyle doesn't even look up.

          He looks
at me.

He pushes the glasses up on his nose and turns back to
work.

          He says,

          Easy, but hungry.

ELEMENTS

1988

The Heart

A stumblebum in scree.

A hummingbird with internal bleeding.

A desert windmill churning out
Its painful water,
Gurgling *like, like, like.*

This must be the pursuit of happiness,
Which is no one's right.

A game the heart plays hurting.

A butterfly with sore feet.

The windowstunned bird willing
To batter itself further
For its birthright the air.

Someone reciting an original poem
With his throat cut.

Testimony

You can't step into the same
River even once,
And why would you want to? You can't
Lie down without turning your back
On someone. The sun slips
Like butter in a pan.

The eastern sky arrives
On the back stoop in its dark
Suit. It draws itself up
Full height to present its double
Rainbow like an armful of flowers.
Thank you, they're lovely.

I step outside where the wind
Lifts my hair and it's just
Beginning to rain in the sun,
And the earth silvers like a river
We're in, I swear to God,
And you can't step out of a river

Either. Not once.

Against the Rest of the Year

The meadow's a dream I'm working to wake to.
The real river flows under the river.
The real river flows
Over the river.
Three fishermen in yellow slickers
Stitch in and out of the willows
And sometimes stand for a long time, facing the water,
Thinking they are not moving.

*

Thoughts akimbo
Or watching the West slip through our hopes for it,
We're here with hay down,
Starting the baler, and a thunderhead
Stands forward to the east like a grail of milk.

*

The sky is cut out for accepting prayers.
Believe me, it takes them all.
Like empty barrels afloat in the trough of a swell
The stupid bales wait in the field.
The wind scatters a handful of yellow leaves
With the same sowing motion it uses for snow.

*

After this we won't be haying anymore.
Lyle is going to concentrate on dying for a while
And then he is going to die.

The tall native grasses will come ripe for cutting
And go uncut, go yellow and buckle under snow
As they did before for thousands of years.
Of objects, the stove will be the coldest in the house.
The kitchen table will be there with its chairs,
Sugar bowl, and half-read library book.
The air will be still from no one breathing.

*

The green of the meadow, the green willows,
The green pines, the green roof, the water
Clear as air where it unfurls over the beaver dam
Like it isn't moving.

*

In the huge secrecy of the leaning barn
We pile the bodies of millions of grasses,
Where it's dark as a church
And the air is the haydust that was a hundred years.
The tin roof's a marimba band and the afternoon goes dark.
Hay hooks clink into a bucket and nest.
Someone lifts his boot to the running board and rests.
Someone lights a cigarette.
Someone dangles his legs off the back of the flatbed
And holds, between his knees, his hands,
As if they weighed fifty pounds.
Forever comes to mind, and peaks where the snow stays.

Sociology

A small white
Envelope appeared under the door
And it was the beginning of the world.

No one opened it
Which brings us to the present.

A fly hits the windowscreen
Like a distant pistol shot.

We fall asleep

And the story being read us
Keeps going,

About an otherwise young man
Who turns suddenly white

While buying an orange on the street.

Paradise of ashes, fragrant nights,
The sun doesn't know what time it is
Or up from down.

Don't cry,

In the story it is nice out
And they eat some soup.
Under the door

A small white envelope appears
And they open it.

The Story of the End of the Story

To keep from ending
The story does everything it can,
Careful not to overvalue
Perfection or undervalue
Perfect chance,
As I am careful not to do in telling.
By now a lot has happened:
Bridges under the water,
No time outs,
Sinewy voices from under the earth
Braiding and going straight up
In a faint line.
I modify to simplify,
Complicate to clarify.
If you want to know your faults, marry.
If you want to know your virtues, die.
Then the heroine,
Who resembles you in certain particulars,
Precipitates the suicide
Of the author, wretchedly obscure,
Of that slim but turgid volume,
By letting slip:
Real events don't have endings,
Only the stories about them do.

Genesis

Not in wilderness to beguile them
But in a garden, which is wilderness beguiled.
Not in reason but in temptation,
Not in compassion but in judgment.
Not for better and not for worse.
Not for an idea.
Not for the atom that cracks, the flower that opens,
Not for the newspaper bursting into flame,
The ultimate nail, driven in. Not for love,
Not on their lives,
Whose relative happiness or virtue
It was not for,
Not for, not for, not for.

Coming into His Shop from a Bright Afternoon

Like a local flurry or stars too small to use that spilled, iron
filings stain the dirt floor silver.
                                   In the center of the floor,
the forge, in the center of the forge, the rose the bellows angers.

He lights a cigarette on rose-colored steel then hammers the
steel over the anvil's snout.
                                   Red sprays of sparks splash from
each strike.
                     One gummy, fly-specked window begins to allow a
sprawl of wrenches, brushes, punches, chisels, taps, gauges…
Coalsmell.
                 Sweat.
                             The distant blue his eyes are.
                                               There is a lathe
and milling machine, both homemade from scraps.
                                               He chooses a
lighter hammer.
                         Now I can read the names on varnish cans and see
how the walls are layered under sawblades, snowshoes, an
airplane propeller, a loom.
                                 On the other side of the door at my back, the
light I came in from grows white like a blizzard or hot steel.

Hammer blows ring across the meadow too much like bells.
                                                       He is
shaping a piece of earth.
                                 He is hammering it into what he wants.
He thrusts it back into the fire when it loses its blush.

Regard

In regard to their own movement
The stars we track have no inkling.
They're just burning.
Is the willow less in winter?
God's a far cry and busy
Counting dead ants, dead stars.
In regard to its own movement the willow tree
Knows less and less.
Now and then now and then
I forget what I am saying
To myself, often
When you touch me,
Even if we are just wandering down this street
On the surface of a planet
Turning through the fire.

Cartography

Out on the border a howl goes up, skinning the cold air.
A windrush as if from enormous wings descending
Slicks the grass down and thumps, and the whole sky bruises.
Out on the border it stops just as suddenly
As if there were some mistake, and there is: mortal beauty
This world can't bear, and a skeletal silence
Administrates the clouds, their passages, their dissolutions in light.

Out on the border right and wrong are more distinct,
But the border itself is suggestive, permissive, a thinly dotted line.
Amassed armies of forests and grasses poise,
Encroach, but never cross.
Even the sky stays on one side.
Another howl goes up, not a threat as was thought,
But an invitation to an interior. The border

Halves a piece of paper into here and hereafter.
A man, himself a fascicle of borders, draws a map and can't stop
    drawing
For fear of bleeding, smudging, disappearance.
When the map is complete the page will be completely
Obscured by detail, then a third howl.
Three things about the border are known:
It's real, it doesn't exist, it's on all the black maps.

Geometry Is the Mind of God

A point is that which has no part.
A line is a breadthless length.
A man in his life is a point on a line:
That which has no part on a breadthless length.
The far horizon is a line made of vanishing points,
Near collision of funneling views,
Flat as a corpse's EKG.
The line to my back
Is a heart attack of granite and ice,
A tumble of similar opposites.
The opposite of a mountain
Is the ocean or the sky
Or an island in the ocean
Or an island in the sky
Or a thorn on the island, growing.
And what regards the reeling firmament
With sympathy?
If the ocean has an island,
If the point has no part,
I'd say it's a green thorn in the heart.

At the Sand Creek Bridge

The path of most insistence
Constrains the creek
Where it spools
And rummages through
Its darkest secrets
And the mooncolored trout revolve.
If it's been a long time coming
It'll be a long time gone.
Or so I think, watching it
Neither hurry nor tarry
Through spills and basins
I used to climb among
With a fly rod between my teeth,
And may again
If life is long.
Now I'm content to idle
The truck on the bridge
As the pines offer
Their shadows to water.
I can still remember
A few things.
The years I wasted fishing
Down here.
Cold rock under fingertips
And the smell of willow early.
The lapidary green
Of the little snake
Who swims like water in water.
The sun getting hotter
On my shoulders,
My feet in the current

Going numb.
Once I stood on the canyon rim
And hurled boulders
One after another down,
To boom and ricochet,
To make the shadows speak.
There was no one anywhere
To hear the canyon's utterance
Or how the quiet rushed back hard
When I stopped,
My loneliness complete,
The smell of gunpowder
In the air.

Druthers

Between permission
and obligation
what light gets in
is sifted fine.
A deep separateness
blesses the evergreens,
ashamed of nothing.
Hardly a day goes by.
The long unlikelihood
suffusing all things
becomes, if left alone,
the same as loneliness.
For instance the kindling
you raked into heaps
by the chopping block,
the rubberbands
you left on doorknobs:
little miracles of sadness,
the order things are in,
a shame.
I never asked
for choices or desire.
I never would have turned.
I'd harvest snow
to live on like the timber does.
Days would go by, restrained.

Left-Handed Poem

I am the self of my former shadow.
There's a forest lost in me.
When I walk there the wind scrapes overhead
Like a river I'm at the bottom of.

The opposite of a river,
This furry ridge nonetheless
Flows away and spills itself onto the prairie,
Or maybe it's a root the high peaks need
To fasten them down.

A hundred miles across the sea that went away,
Now windcarved sandstone and cow-specked pasture,
A single peak, triangular
Like a windmill sail,
Lifts itself into the air
And turns the wheel.

Hollow breath of the high couloirs
Turns the branches to water.
Still, but still loud down here among
So much *knowing what to do*.
I can take a hint.
I walk down onto the plain.
Like a small flame I
Steady myself.

What We Said the Light Said

Mystery moves in God-like ways
Is one of many possibilities
And may be why I'm here without you now.

High clouds bruise and white peaks incarnadine.
Slender tree of muliebrity would be another explanation.

Prairie grass, seductive, luxuriates in amber.
Some other
Scraps of clouds the rain left behind
Hunker down for the night in valleys.

The fencepost's shadow leaps out across the plain
Like the bejeezus
Out of someone.

The mirage becomes an oasis
Is something it might have said.
The first stars creep forward
Like wild children coaxed from the woods.

Love, then, was just a sweeter loneliness
Than this,

Though snowbroken aspen across the meadow
Still catch the latest light like a grove
Of saxophones,
Like you said,

Temporary, like eternity,
Though once,

And once again,
Daylight held us on the tip of its tongue
And forgot what it was saying.

It Just So Happens

You fingered the white top
Button of your white blouse.

I just tried to act natural.
A tree fell in the forest

Nearby without making a sound.
Like most of what we said

It made the silence deeper.
Our laughter made us sadder.

You said the only cure
For anxiety was fear.

Now solitude undoes loneliness
Like a ribbon from your hair,

And the sound at last arrives
That knocks the wind out of the ground.

Combat Zone

Peculiarities of temperament
Variously inform interpretations,
Like a siren setting dogs all over town
Diversely howling, or a man walking through
A hair-trigger wheatfield.
Choices concerning deployment of desire
Conform to shapely patterns known as doom.
I don't care who you are.
Whole galaxies of possibility
Smear and dry on the curled floor tiles
Of the peepshow booth.
Someone is still alive in the trenches,
Appalled by a stale loneliness,
Dying of meanings,
Enduring for love's say-so.

What wouldn't you do?

Easy Riddle

It's a nail of black water driven deep
And broken off deep in.
It's a lens that stars resolve in,
Like a telescope so strong
It sees through the earth's center, sees stars
On the far side
More imaginable, somehow, than those above,
And the last cigarette
In your delicate and mortal hand
Traverses that heaven
Again and again like a lovesick planet without a hunch
How black the nail, how deep the water,
Holding these reflections up to us.

Holy Saturday, An Exercise in Personification

The jetstream lost its grip and rose
Trailing snowhungry Sonoran air
For a month, like refugees,
But too easy, unbelievable.
Pasqueflowers disinterred themselves
Early for the earliest Easter in memory.
For delighters in irony
As the only intelligent, and hence
Predictable, virtue of weather,
The foot of snow,
Expected, followed. The flowers
Close up now, but without terror,
Buried alive again
In a tangible atmosphere of purity.
A prairie of flowers inside a prairie of snow!
They do not ask.
They do not mention the word *forsaken*.
Why should they,
Who have nothing to do but wait and see.

Black Star

No windows in heaven though –
A pat on the back never over.

Was that a gunshot or did someone drop a broom?
Is it the wind or someone sweeping?

Skittish rainclouds glance off the jetstream like seraphic horses
And every day is the provisional ending

So every day the blue spruce float their ridges
To the edge of the sky and wait.

The afterlife will be the same
But without anger. God will be closer

And still too far.

Justice

All around the house huge elms and oaks
Billow up like green thunderheads
In heat that brings cicadas to a boil.
You might think no one's died for a while.
The air is still
Until the tousled willow stirs
From a deeply sexual nap,
And a slight wind
Flips through a paperback
Left open near the open window.
From the way it skims I'd say
This breeze has no interest in the text.
It's looking for some tiny flowers
And four-leaf clovers it would like to have back.
So I take down a notebook I know to be full
Of such flowers and clovers
My mother gathered during her life
Of trying to make the ephemeral last,
And open it near the open window
For the wind to leaf through
And want what it takes.

Sentences for a Friend Snowed In

His snowfences are sentences
Of braille the wind can read,
Though sometimes it ignores his suggestions.

The snowfence is not a fence.

It discontinues,
Contains without surrounding,
Makes the sound of one hand praying.

It holds back the snow by letting it through
And holding back the wind.

Now that Lyle lives alone
His snowfences are fears that say
What he doesn't want to happen.

He doesn't want to be overwhelmed.

He doesn't want to go down,
Snow rising past the windows.

What if the wind indeed prevails?

Spindrift imitates the soul held down,
And the snowfence is a wooden spine that dreams.

The other hand?

Inside – tending the fire.

Synopsis of a Failed Poem

Every simile is elegy,
Resolving in eternal principles.

The axioms are natural, the rules
Are sentimental. Habit animates

The animate, shapely patternings
Accumulate, more awkward to shoulder than trees.

Though not for fear now, images demure.
The lines descend like snow-blind mountaineers.

To the Republic

                                                    Past
fences the first sheepmen cast across the land, processions
of cringing pitch or cedar posts pulling into the vanishing
point like fretboards carrying barbed melodies, windharp
narratives, songs of *place*, I'm thinking of the long cowboy
ballads Ray taught me the beginnings of and would have taught
me the ends if he could have remembered them.

                                        But remembering
was years ago when Ray swamped for ranches at a dollar a day
and found, and played guitar in a Saturday night band, and now
he is dead and I'm remembering near the end when he just needed
a drink before he could tie his shoes.

                                    We'd stay up all night
playing the beginnings of songs like *Falling Leaf*, about a
girl who died of grief, and *Zebra Dun*, about a horse that
pawed the light out of the moon.

                                    Sometimes Ray would break
through and recall a few more verses before he'd drop a line
or scramble a rhyme or just go blank, and his workfat hands
would drop the chords and fall away in disbelief.

                                                Between
songs he'd pull on the rum or unleash coughing fits that
sounded like nails in a paper bag.

                                        Done, he'd straighten and
say, *My cough's not just right, I need another cigarette*, and
light the Parliament he bit at an upward angle like Roosevelt
and play the start of another song.

                                    Then, played out and
drunk enough to go home, he'd pick up his hat and case and
make it, usually on the second try, through the front gate
and gently list out into the early morning dark, beginning
again some song without end, yodeling his vote under spangles.

Matins

Dawn comes on hard and the peaks take one step back.
Planetary residue eddies in the angling light.
A horse stomps in the yard.
What's it to you?

To apprehend perfection is
To presuppose intention, and we do.
The poem is richer for the writer since
It's my horse.

And it's my neighbor, Frank, in the hospital this time.
Death makes us possessive, I guess.
Its expressiveness depends on imperfection,
Which in turn depends on notions of perfection

Sufficiently out of reach
To prove illusive: *I've known him all my life.*
Roger drives out to bring the cows down for winter
Since Frank is in the hospital.

I see Roger coming ten miles away, pulling horses,
Raising a horsetail of dust at least a mile long
That sizzles down the road
Like a burning fuse.

Grief's Aspect

The cemetery is just a melancholy
Marina and rain
Is the tallest girl I know.

Lookit.
A new slip.
The lawn pulls and swells.

What's amazing is
How manageable it makes us,
As if we were pulling

Over for a siren.
That's why sirens mourn in advance
For what happens.

Special Effects

My shirts on the line
(One sleeve has fondly blown
Around its neighbor's shoulders)
Look like drunks at a funeral.

Raindrops open parachutes
Shading off to snow.

The back fence leans in
And curves down like a breaking wave.

Beyond it
The slender lodgepole pines
Stand so close together
You couldn't walk through them
In your body.

Meteorology

The heart is such a big awkward girl,
I think it's a paper cup of gasoline.
The floor dozes off when I walk across it,
And the windows turn opaque
When they are sure no one is around.

At night when no one sees them
Lovers write each other's names
With black volcanic stones
On the white salt flats.
There were slamming doors and flowers,

A cup of milk left on the stove too long.
There was all the wind in Wyoming.
No one saw anything.
We were not evil enough to make decisions,
But able to let things happen

Evil enough.
We are learning that weather
Is always merciless –
Even if you don't mean weather –
Even the best days.

Materialism

If things aren't things
So much as happenings,
Or a confluence even
More complex,
Then there's no such thing
As sky, though sky
Is real, and we
Have not imagined it.
The everlasting
Never began.
Everything, then,
Is the direction everything
Moves in, seeming
Not to move.
I am waiting
For something very
Nice to happen,
And then it happens:
Your long dark
Hair sweeps
Across my chest
Like sweeps of prairie
Rain. Loveliest
Of motion's possessions,
Hold me still.

Avatar

The imperceptible
Becomes something
Like geese flying,
Or sometimes you hear
A girl's name, that's all.

In many syllogisms
Which begin with words
Like *if morality*,
Narcissism and possibly
Wheelchairs are dignified.

According to a man
Who writes near urinals
In Arcata, California,
The meek don't want it.
And across the street

In another bar,
In the same delirious
Hand and green
Felt-tipped pen,
Thelma, do what thou wilt.

Emptiness makes
The world occur more,
Causing love and problems.
The imperceptible
Becomes something

And there you are.

Life Throes

Funny wind,
The grass bends over laughing.
This is a dream you could photograph or die of,
A dream you could nail to a tree.

Because it never ends
I call it *when you leave me*;

Because it never begins
I call it *how I found you*.

I call it *unlike the other small*
When a trout leaps
At a handtied fly
Snagged on a low willow branch.

The fish becomes the willow's ornament.
The fisherman is never seen again,

Not in this dream.
Funny wind.

When you leave home, home leaves with you,
Turtle, turtledove.

It was ever so.
As soon as I look back to see
What's unbelievably
Following still,

As soon as I wave at what I believe in,
It's this dream again,

The one without you.

Spring Blizzard

A limb's sententious crack
Is its apology for breaking.

Far enough is far enough for once.

When we mention *the world*,
We mean our fate before we know it.

I broke as you were mentioning the world.

This is how the moon feels
Whose orbit snaps in apogee.

I wish you wouldn't look at me that way.

My Death as a Girl I Knew

I was in a story

In the middle of a field of tall grass
Like someone in a story would
For no reason

It was just as green
It was just as many

When one seedtop brushed another
They both rushed to say
Excuse me quite all right

I smelled music in the piano bench
Gun solvent
A woman's pillow

My sister calls and calls
And I still don't
I like it here when I don't

Let them

Tapping of the wedge and hammer
Father splitting the tree
The tree that split the rock

The rock that spoke
That split in two for the tree

Once

A Safe Place

Because wind is architecture
Independent for its meaning
On any sense of ending,
And light modifies as it asserts,

The hour an angle, a topspin
To get along, on the wire cutters for instance,
The chrome ones I left on your *Essential Horace*,
And because it isn't early anymore mornings

I thought to trace
A windy architecture, circular by nature,
Shot with resolution, because I need a safe place
To keep the wire cutters, here.

And while I'm at it I'm putting in
The angle of your wrist as you draw back from your
Brow that sunstruck auburn hair,
And the way you clear your throat

As if you were about to say something
But then you don't say anything.

Not So Much on the Land as in the Wind

Not so much on the land as in the wind,
From where I stand the nearest tree is blue.
The house is log and built to last. It has –
Past the souls who tried to make a life here.
One huge overshoe and a galaxy
Of half-moons gouged into linoleum
Where someone's father tipped back in his chair
To formulate plain thoughts and then to speak
In counterpoint to the wind's sad undersong.
He knew the wind was grinding his life away.
Now roof nails bristle obscenely where shingles have flown,
And the blown-out panes all breathe astonishment.
The leaning barn is only empty sort of.
It harbors rows of cool and musty stalls. Dark stalls
That haven't held a dreaming horse in years.
I turn to leave, turn back to latch the gate –
Odds on the past to outlast everything –
I walk toward the tree to make it green.

Driving into Laramie

Out here sheer force of sky bearing down
Could crush the town to dust and hand it back.

So it lies low in cringing boxiness
And draws back, as if it didn't know them,
From its own absurdly wide streets,
Which are stupid promises
Where nothing lingers the wind would linger over.

The steeple of the Episcopal church
And the obsolete smokestack at Monolith Portland
Insult the sunshot blue above the leveled town,
The one a washed-out dream prosperity woke from,

The other, in this whereabouts, a reflection in the sky
Of the hard thorn in every citizen,
His just belief
That God is impressed above all by defiance.

Death at Work

A Chevy engine hangs by a chain
From a limb of the spreading ponderosa.

The toolshed smells of stale blood
And is padlocked.

Trying not to be afraid explains everything.

A riding boot slit down both seams
Lolls behind the open door.

The rising sun peeks under cloud cover
As if for purposes of identification
And then disappears for the day.

Hush now,
I promise not to tell any stories
With everyone afraid and trying not to be.

About

Facts about the iris
Do not make the iris
Open. Open your eyes.
It's tomorrow: Call out for someone.

Botany

*for Ray Worster, 1918–1984, who died of freezing
on Boulder Ridge, where he was born*

Shuteye rifted by unspeakables,
All manner of failure to be glad
Returns the inward stare, the tendency…
The tendency of tall notions to fall short,
Small relationships of things to people,
Ray's smokes on the windowsill, for example, to fall
Away and leave their terrible impressions
Here.

The work we do is suffer the above,
As if witness changed what we witness, changed us,
As if the reason we must change were no
More than the rumor of a desert flower
We could not find and so could not betray.

Reading the Will

The violins are doing their laundry.
The world turns on a nail.
This failure has no intention of turning back.
Abstractions like *eschatology*

Consume themselves before becoming.
When accused of theosophy I always maintain
I didn't really mean it,
Even if I mean I didn't really do it.

Imagination is that around which
Mysteries assemble for devotion.
It believes everything, even reason,
Which denies everything. Pay Attention.

My mother willed me her binoculars –
So I still might see her that far away?
Also her silver hairbrush
And other celebrations of anguish.

The durable, once gone, is gone for good.
The ephemeral lasts and lasts.
Abstractions like *eschatology* last and last.
All borders are the signature of fear. Pay Attention.

My mother painted her lips bright red
And held a drop of honey on her tongue.
Hummingbirds kissed her and drank there.
The world turns on a nail.

The Uncertainty Principle

The real is not what happens but what is
About to happen,

Whatever you were dying for before.

Knowing is just feeling
With a sense of direction, and
Thinking tags after like a string of tin cans

Annoying everyone.
Something was about to happen.
Really.

My mother said I'd never make it back
In time by the way she looked at me forever.

She wasn't thinking.

I pledge allegiance to her eyes,
Don't envy me.

When you reach the North Pole the idea of north
Becomes unrealized, free.

Which north was true?
Which south was home?
What is it you are dying for?

Only the stars, which do not know, can tell,
Only the stars, which do not know, can tell.

No

There are no proofs
Only witnesses,
No evidence or guilt,
But crimes…occurrences…
Victims, including everyone.
Beyond the conception
Of redemption,
No redemption,
No quivering Jesus.
Roadmaps grow on trees.
What do you want me to be?
Among witnesses, I mean.

Trapper's Cabin

Green fire burning the snow is just the woods in time lapse,
the way God sees them.

Beavers make mirrors out of freshets,
stob the mountain's bleeders.

All a beaver wants out of life
is a burglar alarm made from still water, and a sense of *been*
and *going* when he goes.

Grass chokes down.

The dead ponds are
living meadows that start to bleed again.

In the middle of the
meadow a man fashioned a shelter of trees and mud, log ends
axed off sharp, the way the beavers leave them.

He set his traps
and tried to live awhile, enough.

Many years after he was done
(I was alive by then) three old ladies, strangers, drove up in
a yellow car, a Hudson, and cleaned the place out – bent chairs,
blue enamel washbasins, medicine bottles blued by sun.

Then the
roof fell in.

Then beavers dammed the creek again.

Imagine the
log shack weathered silver in the middle of the silver pond –
not on an island, mind you, right on the water, floorboards
barely clear.

Where someone lived and doesn't.

If beavers had
a king, this would be his castle.

In time lapse, the way God
sees things, it would look like everything – water, grass, house,

water – succeeded out of the ground to be held unharmed in cold, green flame.

The man whose life awhile this was appears as a dull aura the cabin has at first, like an electron cloud, that dully glows and dims.

Post-Modernism

A pinup of Rita Hayworth was taped
To the bomb that fell on Hiroshima.
The avant-garde makes me weep with boredom.
Horses *are* wishes, especially dark ones.

That's why twitches and fences.
That's why switches and spurs.
That's why the idiom of betrayal.
They forgive us.

Their windswayed manes and tails,
Their eyes,
Affront the winterscrubbed prairie
With gentleness.

They live in both worlds and forgive us.
I'll give you a hint: the wind in fits and starts.
Like schoolchildren when the teacher walks in,
The aspens jostle for their places

And fall still.
A delirium of ridges breaks in a blue streak:
A confusion of means
Saved from annihilation

By catastrophe.
A horse gallops up to the gate and stops.
The rider dismounts.
Do I know him?

LETHAL FREQUENCIES

1995

Hell to Breakfast

for Steve Adkisson

Stevie, vandals smashed
The fretless you made me I
Hear it

Independence Day, 1956, A Fairy Tale

I think this house's mouth is full of dirt.

Smoke is nothing up its sleeve.

I think it could explode.

Where I am, in the dirt under the floor, I hear them.

They don't know.

My mother leaves each room my father enters.

Now she is cleaning things that are already clean.

My father is in the living room.

He's pouring.

Rum into a glass, gas into a lamp, kerosene into a can. He pours capped fuses, matches, dynamite sticks into his pockets.

He pours rounds into the .45 which he will point skyward and hold next to his ear as if it were telling him things.

Where I am, the spider spins.

The broken mouse drags a trap through lunar talc of dust.

Where the bitch whelps is where I wriggle on my belly, cowardly, ashamed, to escape the Fourth of July.

I think the house is very ready.

It seems to hover like an "exploded view" in a repair manual.

Parts suspended in disbelief.

Nails pulled back, aimed.

My father goes out.

My mother whimpers.

                              There'll be no supper.
She opens the firebox and stuffs it full of forks.

The Weather Spider

1.

A spider lives in the barometer.
It's a white spider and it was born there.

Sometimes it rains from a clear blue sky.
Or rain falls without touching the ground.

Or it doesn't rain.
Of course we had weather before the spider,

Before the barometer, so it isn't that.
We have thunder in winter, dry lightning

Unraveling the tree and the three good horses under it,
Snow leaving the earth and

Falling straight up, back into the cloud.
Anybody got a match?

Anybody got a thimbleful of blood?

2.

After a slim night storm
The spidery likenesses of aspens
Memorize the north sides

Of the trees themselves.
Wouldn't it be wrong to say
The new buds *wait*, sheathed in ice?

Do you think the spider doesn't *matter* to weather
Just because it lives in the barometer?
The first light seems to like it

In these glass branches.
The whole morning is given
To unilateral disarmament

Of all sides.
Beneath the glass
The spider's indifference towards us

Grows immense, indomitable.
Anybody got a thimbleful of blood?

Art Class

Let us begin with a simple line,
Drawn as a child would draw it,
to indicate the horizon,

More real than the real horizon,
Which is less than line,
Which is visible abstraction, a ratio.

The line ravishes the page with implications
Of white earth, white sky!

The horizon moves as we move,
Making us feel central.
But the horizon is an empty shell –

Strange radius whose center is peripheral.
As the horizon draws us on, withdrawing,
The line draws us in,

Requiring further lines,
Engendering curves, verticals, diagonals,
Urging shades, shapes, figures…

What should we place, in all good faith,
On the horizon? A stone?
An empty chair? A submarine?

Take your time. Take it easy.
The horizon will not stop abstracting us.

On Exploration

A hawk drops to the treetop
Like a falling cross.
The haybarn is ticking.
The Universe has everything.
That's what I like about it.
A single chubby cloud
Beelines downwind
Trying to catch up with the others.

Yellow leaves plane across the water,
Drifting the inlet.
The pond is a droozy eye.
Details tend to equal each other,
Making decisions harder.
Is polio an endangered species?
The Universe is mostly empty,
That's important;
A fractal palindrome of concentric

Emptinesses.
Is there life out there?
Are there lawns?
Columbus is famous for discovering a place
Where there were already people
Killing each other.
Nothing missing. Nothing new.

Let's pick wildflowers.
Let's take a meteor shower.
Let's live forever and let's die, too.

Two Horses and a Dog

Without external reference,
The world presents itself
In perfect clarity.

Wherewithal, arrested moments,
The throes of demystification,
Morality as nothing more
Than humility and honesty, a salty measure.

Then it was a cold snap,
Weather turned lethal so it was easier
To feel affinity
With lodgepole stands, rifted aspens,
And grim, tenacious sage.

History accelerates till it misses the turns.
Wars are shorter now
Just to fit into it.

One day you know you are no longer young
Because you've stopped loving your own desperation.
You change *life* to *loneliness* in your mind
And, you know, you need to change it back.

Statistics show that
One in every five
Women
Is essential to my survival.

My daughter asks how wide is lightning.
That depends, but I don't know on what.

Probably the dimension of inner hugeness,
As in a speck of dirt.

It was an honor to suffer humiliation and refusal.
Shame was an honor.
It was an honor to freeze your ass horseback
In the year's first blizzard,
Looking for strays that never materialized.

It was an honor to break apart against this,
An honor to fail at well-being
As the high peaks accepted the first snow –
A sigh of relief.

Time stands still
And we and things go whizzing past it,
Queasy and lonely,
Wearing dogtags with scripture on them.

Listen Hard

Enough and you can hear
The small breakages occurring.
That's what all sounds are:
Small sounds, small things breaking;
Big sounds, big things breaking.

Think of a drop of water
Flung from the grindstone.
It's always day, it's always night.
No such thing as tomorrow.

There's a match going out.
There's paying for privilege.
There's harm's way,

It's all the same day.
Sunlight drools on the grass.
An air of faded intimacy.

Listen to the sound of the pages turning.
Listen to the sound of the book when it closes.

A Portrait of My Roof

My steel roof mirrors clouds
Like a book the sky left off reading.

The story of clouds passing keeps passing,
As stories will, even with the book turned over,

Even closed, shelved, forgotten;
Inside I leave off working

And turn my notebook spine up to wonder
What kind of story is boring the sky.

I don't have to go far for the answer.
I don't have to go anywhere.

Shall I take up serpents for interest?
I have taken up serpents.

Shall I refuse happiness?
For interest?

No, I shall claim the obvious,
That hearts are no exclusive province.

I shall go outside and lie down in the grass.
I shall read the passing clouds,

Chaotic, senseless, wise,
Unlike anything one finds in reflection.

More Like It

1.

It's white ashes
That drift and mizzle,
Muffle and sift like snow.

Feather-ash, not snow.
Sure sign Heaven
Has burned to the ground again.

The pines
(Ah, Unanimous!)
Elect a new God.

2.

The jetstream careens
As if with a new God at the wheel.

The pines never stop praying.
They pray best in a drizzle.

The pines pray up a drought.
They pray snowdrifts and sheet lightning.

They get everything they pray for.
They get sex with the wind.

3.

Pine pollen yellows the air
Thick as smoke.
Woodgrain flames inside the pines,
Insatiable, flames
Like palms pressed together.

4.

Here in pines under ashen sky
I am. Reason is
To join my prayers
With theirs.

The War That Isn't What You Think

The little wind I saw curving and lifting
The black mare's mane
Never came this way,
Though I waited, face tilted:
To wind as heliotropic is to sun.

We have to keep our disappointment alive.
We have to sustain our appal, act surprised
That humanity has (again today!)
Failed to evolve away from meanness.
That we ourselves have failed in this.

Invisible earth,
I still can't feel any wind,
Can't feel though I hear cottonwood leaves that hung still
Turn sudden, turn all-at-once,
Like small birds in a flight of small birds, turning,

Like one thing instead of many,
Turn silver side to the wind when it comes,
Shiver and moan when it comes.
O wind, immaculate, that lifts the mane,
Immaculate, that turns the silver leaves,
That bears away the smoke of sacrifice.

The wind, when it finds me, bears no trace
Of sage-sweet horsesmell, no color black,
No softness of muzzle of the
Mare, her mane curving and lifting,
Where she grazes the horizon down to nothing.

One Day

For all intents and purposes
The President is folded away for the night.

It's been a bad day
For intents and purposes.

After all is said and done
No one should have said anything.

We should have done otherwise.
It was a terrible day for saying and doing.

People with spectacles were asked to stand forward.
Owls went up in smoke.

What could anyone do about evil or suffering
On a day like this.

Dogs howled in pain from a lethal frequency.
Lovers fell silent and drifted into separate distances.

It was a day, oh – everywhere you turned
A molten angel stood in the way.

I Looked for Life and Did a Shadow See

Some little splinter
Of shadow purls
And weals down
The slewed stone
Chapel steps,
Slinks along
The riverrock wall
And disappears
Into the light.
Now ropy, riffled,
Now owlish, sere,
It smolders back
To sight beneath
A dwarfish, brindled tree
That chimes and sifts
And resurrects
In something's sweet
And lethal breath.
This little shadow
Seems to know
(How can it know?
How can it not?)
Just when to flinch
Just where to loop and sag
And skitter down,
Just what to squirrel
And what to squander till
The light it lacks
Bleeds it back
And finds
My sleeping dark-haired girl –

O personal,
Impersonal,
Continual thrall –
And hammocks blue
In the hollows of her eyes.

Indirective

The ridge road takes the ridgespine every way
It turns. It threads the granite vertebrae
And old, wind-dwarfed ponderosas that twist
Out of the ungiving, unforgiving ground
Like tips of auger bits drilled through from Hell.
Here, all trees die by lightning soon or late.
This hidden side-trail elk hunters found will fall
To their camp on Sheep Creek, where the creek stops them.
They ignite their Colemans, dress the carcasses,
Make drunk display in artificial light.
Years past the road kept going, forded there.
Now the creek has cut and caved the bank.
You have to go on horseback or afoot.
Well, just as well. Afoot or horseback was
The only way to go before the road,
Before the reason for the road arrived,
Disguised as some old trapper, moonshiner,
Xenophobe, or who the hell he was –
Old badger, anyway, who cleared some trees,
Cut some sidehill and creekbank with a slip
And mule to get a wagon way in there
With stores to keep him winterlong and when
The water rose too high to ford, Lord knows.
I said I'd take you there but I don't know.
More than likely I'll just get us lost.
The last time I tried to find the old homestead
I poked around for it awhile and then
Rode on to look for some of Richard's strays.
I never saw a cow that day either.
But I'll take you up and we can look
If your heart's set on it. The only time

I saw the place myself I was with Ray.
Well, now Ray's dead, but he knew where it was,
Back then you could still drive there four-wheel-drive,
Before the crossing disappeared. Even
Then the bank was steep for Ray's old Scout.
We lost the clutch, but Ray still got us there.
The nearby spring doesn't give it away,
Popping out like it does from solid
Rock, where even willows will not grow,
And diving underground before you know it,
As if it didn't like it here above.
What it looks like, in case we come up empty,
It looks small, just part of the woods, but small,
The cabin I mean, its logs obscured by brush.
It's dwarfed by the size of trunks surrounding it.
Deep snow country grows big trees. They vault
And loom in shadowed unconcern. The cabin
Is squalid, yes, but mostly it looks dim,
Or maybe brief would be the way to say it –
Depressing brevity we recognize
As squalor. Not much sun in woods like those,
None inside the windowless log shack.
Let's touch our horses up across this park.
That grove yonder might just be the one.
That time I came up here with Ray, God rest,
The time we found the place – it's only six
Or seven logs in height and ten-feet square –
The door was ajar and stingy with its dark.
I noticed that before I saw the roof
Caved in, which made that depth of dark seem strange.
It kind of chilled me when we found the spine
Of something human-sized right by the door.
Ray mentioned, *There's no need to close the door*
Behind you if you're going out to die.
It was half-buried. I'm not saying it

Was a man, just that it could have been.
I wouldn't know a spine of bear from man
Or woman, would you? I'll be damned. We're here.
It all looks just the same. The spine is gone.
What's that? A skull, sure as hell, half-buried,
Or half-unburied, like a blind white eye
In the ground. Relax. It isn't human.
More like an old badger. See the teeth? Here
The only human bones are yours and mine.

Sapphic Suicide Note

day out
no worldly joy
italics mine

Speaking Terms

All around me to-ing and fro-ing
In a strapping south wind
Pine boughs lisp their approval
Of moving without moving around, saying,
Shh! This way! Shh! This way!
They contradict each other
By all saying the same thing.

Better to impersonate than to
Personify, when it comes to nature.
Shh! I tell them. This way!
And start walking.

Trespassers

Now, on this new page,
A new optimism groans into place.
The leaves, like extras
One is beginning to know by name,
Sigh and lift perceptibly.
A doe steps into the clearing and looks toward the house –
Just checking – then turns and highsteps
With exaggerated precision, flight held in,
Back to cover.
Two hunters,
Trespassing but willing to claim
They are lost, mistaken, sorry,
Simmer in the throaty idle of their pickup,
Gazing down into a deep draw.
They pull away slowly. They'll be back.
The day itself is good.
Whatever happens in the day,
The day itself is good.
A breeze tensely riffles the pond,
Erasing the pond's attempt at representation
Of treetops and sky – try again.
It keeps doing that.
A jet goes over and you rise to build a fire.
As if the jet were a signal.
One hunter says good day, though,
Even if we don't get anything.
Nice weather.
And the deer step out of the woods
As if drawn by a magnet.

Right Now

The Mind assumes The Position
Under a cocaine moon.
Flip.
Live it up.
De-tox, re-tox, just like tides.
Shouldn'a, wouldn'a.
Ifn't.
There is no shadow without a field
To fall on.
Tomorrow we can say, "Tomorrow."
Don't tell me the truth will set you free.
It's too busy making you a hero.
As for critics, they don't know.
They'll never know. They're not supposed to know.
Acedia aside,
Acceptance is the only way that grace survives.
In us.
Us shadows with no field to fall on.
The violins were slobbering.
There were heavy buildings.
There were plenty of anxious people, crying,
"That men may not forget me utterly."
So there was a bonfire made of oars.
There was.
Without you I'd be heartless.
I'd say, "Be there when it all goes wrong!"
I might be stupid but I ain't slow.
I don't believe in a world
You could lose in a heartbeat.

Resurrection Update

And then it happened.
Amidst cosmic busting and booming
Gravity snapped,
That galactic rack and pinion.

Trees took off like rockets.
Cemeteries exploded.
The living and the dead
Flew straight up together.

Only up was gone. Up was away.
Earth still spun
As it stalled and drifted darkward,
Sublime,

An aspirin in a glass of water.

Untitled, 1968

for Mark Rothko

There's no such thing as an emergency.

                              Betrayal is eventual.

The bridge is a river, when you think about it.

                                     River of blood,

when you think about it.

                    The Lord giveth.

                              Highest echelons of

quietude.

          A veronica in each sunset.

                        In every blackening bandage

in the hospital's unspeakable bins, a veronica.

                         Someone suffered

here.

    The elevator full of blood rose like any other.

                              Why not.

Our nets were full of sunset when we hauled them in.

                           The red sail

filled and pulled us darkward.

                Blood in the drumroll blossomed.

The Lord giveth.

         Thou shalt.

                Change the bandages when they blacken.

Don't think about it.

         Set the red sail and disappear.

                        Slow drip

in silence.

     Don't say a word.

             Don't say the wineglass on the sill

is a sun-dried Sangreal.

It's a landscape.
You just can't bring
your body.
The bridge is an inward horizon.
The bridge has arrived
in time for us to cross.
I know because someone, or his assistant,
suffered here.

You Know What People Say

Sulky what-ifs.
Sulky what-ifs.
They bumblefuck the metastuff.
Diffidence their stock in trade.
Cozy hell – cozy, hell.
They make a mockery of irony.
They hold Special Olympics in wit.
What was Shakespeare's blood pressure?
Vertical river, cloister of thunder,
Bleeds the ship's fell sail.
God comes in for a landing. He lowers God's landing gear.
He raises the holy spoilers, lowers the sacred ailerons. He imagines
Reality.
Tried everything in life?
Sulky what-ifs are dumbstruck. Drumsticks.
Their spiritual actuality is empirical.
What if uppity angels?
What if there really were rules?
What if those angels melted in the rain?
If reality is illusion, wouldn't it stand to reason
That illusions are real?
A lot of dumb questions.
Impingement of external objects or conditions upon the body
Palpitate apostasy.
The oppressed must free the oppressors to free themselves, see?
The soul is euphemism for the body.
What does *willing* mean? Do you sense my sense?
Am I fashionable?
Objective as an angel in the rain?
Screaming from a safe place?
Nine smocked doctors, three unmasked.

One has left his face sewn to the pillow.
One holds a lace fan like a hand of cards she studies,
Considering the risks.
She is the loveliest doctor.
Her doctor-father scolds her right there in front of all the other
doctors.
They are aghast.
They kneel and don carnival hats with feathers.
I don't think they are really doctors.
The trees are real. They are green kachinas.
Dark rooms of wind are installed in the house of barbarism.
The norm is always incorrect. If what?

Rubber Angel

The world is not
Your philosophical problem.

Generous with rigor,
Bright blue regardless of heat,

It flourishes in distance.

The flowers we preserved,
The owl-pocked forests
We defended with spikes.

Just try
Not living your life.
I dare you.

The Other Reason It Rains, Etc.

for Ray Worster (1918–1984) and Lyle Van Waning (1922–1988)

It's going to rain for two reasons.
What do you think the other one is.
Time was there was more room

For things to exist:
Price tags, eyebrows, nuns, dungarees,
surf, weeds, eclipses, radios,

Squirrels, sod, junk, siestas.
Yes there was aspirin. Yes there were cellos.
Yes there was brooding tenderness.

That was when there was haying.
I saw Ray's truck parked next to Lyle's,
Bales in the field, three tractors

And the flatbed idle.
To the east God's anvil about to fall through the floor.
Then I saw those two old friends

Across the creek on the hill
Picking wildflowers.
That was when there were pocket combs and willows,

Rain promise, hay down, time in a stitch.
I picked up bales and drove them to the barn,
Which was like a seed of early night

Inside the late afternoon.

Small Countries

In defense of whatever happens next, the navy of flat-bottomed pop-corn clouds steams over like they are floating down a river we're un-der. To the west, red cliffs, more pasture, the blue Medicine Bow with stretchmarked snowfields, quartzite faces like sunny bone. I'm worried about Lyle getting back from town with his oxygen, but then I see him through binoculars turn the Studebaker, antlike, off the county road and up the four-mile grade, so small down there that I want to imagine his hands on the wheel, still strong, his creased blue jeans and high-top shoes I know he wears to town. He turns off the road on a small knoll about halfway up and stops the truck, facing the mountains. He still looks small against so much space, but I can see his left arm and shoulder and the brim of his hat lowered as he lights a smoke and looks off toward the mountains, and small countries of light and dark rush across the prairie towards him and over him.

Big Thompson Svaha

Down from the weary, steeply buttressed cirques,
Over snowfat stands of evergreens,
The river gathers rain into her skirts
And hurries it away. Smithereens
Of broken mountains blush and steam and yawn.
There is no word in English for the gap
Between the look of lightning and its clap:
After a moment of deep consideration,

Permission to resume our lives again.
Tomorrow they will pick limp fishermen
From limbs of trees that never meant to bear,
And oldsters from Dubuque will point to where
Their cottage went, while unexploded propane
Tanks bob, nudge, and spin, so unashamed
In the deep, permissionless consideration
That waits for us, birthlight, deathroll, taken.

Real Wonder

In the stunned little interval
Between winter and spring,
Like the held gasp of surprise
Preceding real wonder,
I'm a flashlight in daylight.

Green stirs low down and shows
Through dead blond shocks of grass,
And gray aspen flowers dangle
Above old snowbanks:
I go around like a feral saint.

The timber hoards
Its meager crust of snow.
I used to walk over the hill
To visit my neighbor
About now.

Just because he was still alive
After another winter.
We'd look out the window
At the groggy meadow,
Not much to say by the end.

This year my neighbor is dead
So I walk the hill anyway.
There's his dead house.
There's his dead fence.
The timber hoards

Its meager crust of snow.
I'm a gunnysack of gravel.
I'm sudden as a gust of light.
This is just
The stunned little interval

After another winter,
The held gasp of surprise
Preceding real wonder.

Emancipation Denunciation

My favorite word today is *delve*,
Which makes a fair showing
In the upper echelons,
Yet is base in origin, like Abraham Lincoln.
Abraham Lincoln delving the earth
In Illinois.

You can do it to anything.
You can't help it.
Your own pocket.
Always delving into something.
Even if only a little.

But today I'm leaving untouched.
I'm writing to keep from meddling in it.
I'm not going to burden this day
With the sadness of doing,
Of having done, irrevocably.

I'm trying to let those few remaining
Yellow aspen leaves
Hang from their aspen branches forever.
The light is aniline in which
The day, too, hangs
In a pause of wrong weather before winter.

Today I'm not building anything
Out of wood, I'm not tearing down
Motors or visiting neighbors.
I'm not putting in the new
Double-hung window.

All blue and gray and bluish gray,
The prairie unfolded under gunmetal sky,
All the green locked away in the pines.
I'm trying to leave the day untouched,
Smooth as a riverstone, one of many,

The amnesia of its surface, *like glass*.

Booklearning

There are certain constants
In Shirley's photographs
Of one-room schools in Albany County, Wyoming.

For one thing,
The schoolmarms are the only ones
Whose clothes ever fit.

A few depict the pale ragamuffins
Horseback, sometimes three or four
Astride the one quixotic nag

That brought them.
One shows the four resident scholars
Perched on the roof of their log Alma Mater,

Massive and gloomy as a wooden raft.
But most are more formulaic:
Children mustered against a wall

To stand in gap-toothed rows,
Wildly varying in height and age, pale
In their tight or tentlike collages of clothes,

Their cowboy hats and galoshes,
Fresh as mushrooms from the logdark where they learned
(Too dim to photograph),

Staring straight into the sun
Of a winter afternoon chosen for its brilliance,
Trying not to blink for long enough.

Indeed these pictures make Albany County
Look much hotter than it is.
The children look like they are burning up

In so much unresisted glare.
Nevermind the snowdrift
Loitering on the right,

Even paler than the squinty grimaces.
When they go back in
They'll all go blind awhile again,

This time in darkness
Where they could see before.
They are learning things

Whose relevance
To the clear light they go home in
Is only promised.

Western Civilization

for William Kittredge

I.

That woman still lives at her ranch.
You can ask her. Maybe
She knows. As near and far

As the rest of us can tell
The barn and sheds were built
In the Great Depression. Someone

Had money and a big idea.
Far and away the biggest
Idea I've ever seen.

Pat says there must've been
A hundred men, shepherds
And shearers, working there.

It's one of those things
That not only is, but seems,
Larger inside than out,

Like a planetarium or an orange,
Even with Wyoming around it,
And real stars flying away.

Just stick your head in there;
Its dark will make you dizzy.
It has an underneath

Too low to stand in unless
You are a sheep. The loft
Vaults like a dusky church.

2.

All that summer
I balanced water,

Coaxing the desert
Into pasture,

With eight cubic feet
Per second for two

Thousand acres.
Horseback, shovel

On my shoulder along
Miles of ditches:

Stalling here,
Releasing there,

Water over
The deepening green,

Keeping it living:
Herons and cranes

Regal in meadows,
Strings of ducklings

Frothing the ditch
To get away.

One day riding ditches I saw Clay.
He was on the hill against the sky,
Flapping his arms at me.
They were going to bulldoze the corrals at the shearing sheds,
Intricate maze of gates and pens
Clay, as a kid, had built with his father,
Before they lost their ranch, before Frank died,
Before the family had to move away.

The new owner was razing everything.
I guess he had some kind of idea.
Clay didn't need any gates, but, as Pat said,
That's Clay.
I met them at the shearing sheds.
Pat held a wrecking bar like a steel snake.
I just can't stand tearin' apart all them guys's dreams,
He said, looking shy.
Hell is when you know where you are.

On the barn roof a loose piece of tin
Flaps in the wind like a broken wing.
Wyoming whirls in the sun.

Up in the loft a pair of shears,
Oh, fifty or sixty years forgotten there,

Floats in noonlight, bearing up some dust,
Just a pair of spring-steel scissors,
Two knives joined at the hip, with smiling edges.

An owl the color of things left alone

Flaps out of the gable door.

Hell is when you know where you are:
Mazes of pens and gates dreaming sheep;
Miles of ditches dreaming green.

5.

No one living knows
Who built the shearing sheds,
Unless maybe that woman,
And I'm not about to ask her,
Ever since she tried
To stab her husband with a pair of scissors.
He was ninety-one
And barely held her off.
Later she claimed she was just
Trying to cut his heart
Medication out of his shirt
Pocket – dope, she called it –
And the old man had to leave
The ranch, where he didn't last long.

They bulldozed the corrals.
We got forty gates.
We took them someplace safe.

6.

Now the vast, dim barn floats like an ocean liner
Whose doldrums are meadows spinning into brush,
And everywhere you look Wyoming hurries off.

All night the stars make their escape.
In the loft a pair of shears cuts woolly moonlight.

All day a piece of roofing slaps in the wind.

A startled owl flaps out of the gable.
Hell is when you know where you are and it's beautiful.
You saved the gates for nothing.

You balanced the water to keep the green from spinning
Away into sage, the same gray as the wing
That just now shaded your eyes.

Rintrah Roars

for John Grant

My father-in-law writes from Umbria (where peasants eat songbirds for lunch and pray beneath frescoes by Giotto): Saturday, 30 Jan. (last day of the season wherein big men can kill little birds).

Lyndon Johnson, while being escorted by a young Marine who said, "That one over there is your helicopter, Sir," replied, placing his arm around the boy, "Son, they're *all* my helicopters."

Sam said, "I might be white bread, but there is one pissed-off nigger in my heart."

McPherson says he doesn't see anything in the world worth coming back for. He wants to get off the wheel, says, "I don't want to come back as anything – not even a bumblebee."

So I say, "Oh, Jim, you'd make a good bumblebee," but I was thinking: That should be enough for anybody's God.

It would be trite to describe the clocksmith's house – the way it sounded like bees in there. "You can never have enough clocks in your house." This from a man who had thousands in his. I asked, "You probably don't even hear them anymore." He said, "I hear them when they stop."

Lyle said, "It's all right to be a fool; it's just not all right to be a old fool."

Steve, the banjo wasn't all they smashed. It was every window. It was every thing I had. You don't want to feel the wind blow through your house that way.

Another friend said, "I am chained to the earth to pay for the freedom of my eyes."

Agriculture

for Richard Borgmann

Tonight the rain can't stand up straight, but once,
Watching over my shoulder the ten wheeling suns
Of the double siderake rolling newmown hay
Over and over and over and over
Into the windrow like a thick green rope,
I was nothing
But a window sailing through the night,
And once when twenty horses wild together
All winter, galloped towards me down the road
With Harrison whooping behind them and
The little stock dog barking at their heels,
And me there to turn them into the corral
From the middle of the road, their eighty
Hooves a roll of thunder in the earth,
Me with a stupid piece of rope in my hand,
I was nothing
But a window sailing through the night.

Expecting Company

Death is when the outside world
Wants to get away from itself
By going inside of someone.

Till the walls cave in.
Till the roof is gone.

I'm floating face up
On a sea of adrenaline.
A broken window hangs around my neck.

I have to make more room in here.
I have to get rid of the furniture.

Winter Road

The reasons the winter road acts so crazy
Are all invisible now.

The summer road persists
In reasoned argument,
Reducing terrain to topography,

Curving gracefully to the left,
Or bending gently to the right,

Gaining, falling, abstracting
Rises, draws, outcrops, woods.

The winter road is crazy.
This time of year it seems
To slam nihilistically

Against the ridgeside,
Sidle through unlikely groves,

Make esses where the summer road goes straight,
Crossing and recrossing,

It dodges to the left, leaps to the right,
A road out of control.

In winter how a road should go
Is told by contours of atmosphere.

The landscape is just a situation
Of windbreaks and wind-permissions.

Heedlessly the summer road
Dives into broad drifts.

It surfaces a couple of times
Between white waves,
Then goes down for good.

Now the winter road is smart to seek
High ground, exposed to wind,

To thread the drifts
Like big white corpses on a field.

Come winter this road proves amazing.
All along it was
In the right place,

Already leaping to the left,
Dodging to the right,

Sailing through contours of atmosphere,
Prophetic and dumb.

Time Optics

Where the ditch vaults the river,
Where the wooden flume weeps over,
Paying the way,
Where its veil makes a thin distance
And has no critics but wind-in-willowshade,
My love and I lay down
In seventeen kinds of native grasses.
We took our time.
Some wasps were building
A Japanese lantern in the branches,
The flume kept weeping into the river.
Chilly ditchwater.
Don't worry, little wasps, wooden flume,
I'll be all right gone.

The Sacral Dreams of Ramon Fernandez

Ramon Fernandez was not intended to be anyone at all.
  — Wallace Stevens

Ramon Fernandez did not live,
As has been suggested,
By the sea.
The unacceptable thoughts
That plagued his dreams
Were diagnosed as being the result
Of unacceptable thoughts.
He could see the stars
Over the San Juan Valley,
Moonlight on the Sangre de Cristo Range.
He could hear,
Despite the constant ringing in his ears,
The feet of *Penitentes*
Scuffing past his low door,
The whistling of their thorn branches.
It all seemed real enough to Ramon,
And not in the least to require his witness.
I'm not saying Ramon Fernandez
Had no imagination.
He could alter the way he saw
Some things, small things,
Like transparent vessels
And birds, both rare and common.
But the mountains were too much for him.
When the *Penitentes* scuffed by moaning,
He hid.

Directly underneath Ramon's fields
An abandoned coal mine smoldered.

It had been abandoned
Because of smoldering.
Every time the wind blew hard
Water in the ditches boiled,
The *acequia* Ramon used
To irrigate his vegetables.
Ramon picked cooked vegetables –
Carrots, turnips, beets –
Out of the steaming soil.
To someone else this might have seemed
Acceptable.
For Ramon it was just the beginning
Of sacral dolor.
For instance,
Ramon Fernandez did not like his father,
Though his father was dying of cancer.
Oh, there were two or three
Paternal qualities
Ramon could list
That might have seemed acceptable
To someone else.
His father was a stoic
To the point of emotionlessness.
His father was a *bultero*.
The *Penitentes* never bothered him!
Then there were Ramon's sisters.
Ramon Fernandez wished
They would leave him alone.
Ramon Fernandez wished they would stop
Praying for him.

His mother had died very young.
Unacceptably young it seemed to Ramon.
It made his ears ring.
He loved his wife and children

With acceptable excess of devotion,
But their mortality –
The idea of it! –
Was unbearable to him.
Furthermore he wanted
To sleep with every woman on earth
Except the ugly ones.
Ramon recognized this feeling
As unacceptable.
When he confessed it to his wife
She made him sleep in the cistern.
Ramon Fernandez it seemed,
Wanted acceptable thoughts
For unacceptable reasons:
To rid himself of chronic lumbar pain,
Gastroenteritis,
Ringing in the ears
And, if possible, to gain
Escape from Hell.

There was, near his house,
On a plateau at the foot
Of the Sangre de Cristo Mountains,
A lake reputed by local myth to be
Unfathomable.
Ramon's solace
Was to lie on the ice at night in winter,
Cruciform, and ponder
The manifest, synchromeshed stars
And the unmanifest
Depths beneath the ice.
He began to think there was only one
Human emotion,
Whose absence was happiness,
Whose anaesthesis was labor,

That loneliness and guilt
Were indistinguishable
Without reference
To the events which triggered them.
The same with love, hate, boredom, nostalgia, envy.

Nostalgia was the worst,
That loneliness for loneliness
That urped over his existence
And immobilized him
With carpal tunnel pain,
Rotator cuff discomfort.
Ramon Fernandez began to think
That all the great philosophers
Were simple fugitives
From the kind of thinking that gives one
Excruciating back pain.
Cowards. Unacceptable.
Especially Nietzsche.
Also Heidegger, Freud, Marx.
All cowards. All had cobbled,
From unacceptable thoughts of loneliness,
Escapes that crumpled like paper wings
On the moonlit talus.
Ramon Fernandez was not sure
About mathematicians
Or astronomers.
He could only guess how lonely
Jesus must have been.

Eventually Ramon unstuck himself
And went home to sleep in the cistern,
Which was onion-shaped, chiseled
Out of solid rock,
Inexplicably dry,

With a single, starry opening at the top.
At least Einstein and (Ramon's favorite)
Wallace Stevens had left
A little room for loneliness,
Had heard what it had to say,
Though a great many poets, it seemed,
Had embraced and later died
Of loneliness,
Like a venereal disease.
Having so thought,
Down in the cistern,
Under the terrifying stars,
Ramon turned to the chiseled wall
And away from desire
For acceptability.
There followed,
Without Ramon's volition
Or reference, images
Of eternal principles –
Not ones he would have thought up
By himself.

For example, his burro.
For example the arias of coyotes
Which never frightened his burro.
For example the asters
His burro stepped on
As they rode, in summer, through the San Juan.
Ramon Fernandez considered the *bultos*
And *santos* his father whittled,
The inherent religiosity
Even of secular art.
He considered the *Penitentes*,
The unbelievable spiritual confusion
Of their children.

He considered the missionary aspect of termites.
When he closed his eyes
He could see the mountains perfectly,
But with eyes closed
He could only approximately
Imagine the stars.
His wrists hurt.
He said, *God has brought me here.*

Woman Walking a One-Kick Dog
Along an Asymptotic Curve

for Bert Honea

Nothing is nothing
Nothing is not nothing
Nothing is next to nothing

Woman Walking a One-Kick Dog
Along an Asymptotic Curve II

I am no one.
I am no one else.

Christmas, 1960

Some of my friends were hoping for BB guns.

I had it over them.

My dad
gave me a .30-.30.

What a great guy.

He gave me ammunition, and when
I fired it, he always stood behind me to catch me when it always knocked
me down.

He was getting me ready to kill a deer that fall.

He taught me
to sit stone-still in a rock outcrop at the bottom of a draw.

He was
going to drive the deer down to me, close enough to kill.

Even a child
could kill that close.

The other thing he taught me was the twenty-
minute nap.

The way you get your sleep in war.

We practiced daily.
Like somebody threw a rock through the window from the outside and
covered the bed with broken glass – that's how I lay next to my father
on the bed while he took his twenty-minute nap, breathing in through
his nose and out through his mouth, and I lay there, light beside him,
under orders.

It wasn't child abuse.

He never touched me.

I would have
levitated if he'd taught me that.

I wasn't napping.

I was not daring

to move for fear he'd wake.

                        I was paying attention to the aspenwood
paneling, the knots like birds' eyes in the ceiling.

                                   Like Ophelia
was how I felt, as the raptors' eyes grew faces, wings.

                                   My face
felt like it was pushing through from the other side of a looking-glass.

Could I have floated, like the dead, I would.

                            But like the living, sank.
The birds with eyes, not all of them friendly, swirled over me.

                                   I saw
a drop of blood at the center of everything.

                         I knew what God was.

                                     I
knew I was my father's little teddy bear of stone.

Postcard

Days are cubes of light
That equal each other
Whether anything happens in them or not,
No matter what anyone did or didn't do,
They are equal.

The emptiest are lovely,
Though one is drawn to the bright-edged shards
Of days that cracked
From disappointment and longing.

Some days I go looking for oceans.
If I find one I search the beach
For the teeth I left
In a glass of water
In a motel room in Nebraska.

I'm losing the ability to tremble.
I find appearances helpful.
Some days I go looking for the sky.

STATIONS

New Poems

Station

Somewhere between a bird's nest and a solar system – whom did
the story use to fashion the crown of thorns, and did it prick
them?

      Whom did the story use for judgement?

                        Whom for betrayal?

The slender filament of drool from too much Quaalude tethered
her chin to her shoulder.

           When I came back she was sitting
on the couch, her hands turned up, her face turned away and down.

Every Annunciation is freaked with doom, flashed in crucifixion.

Because I left home she was allowed to keep pushing her face
through the windshields of collapsing automobiles, as if she
wanted to be born from a speeding car.

               All according to plan,
following the story in telling it.

                  Pilate no more judges Christ
than he judges the air he breathes.

             He is nothing.

                He washes
his hands according to plan, another symbol.

                  It would be like
judging a cloud formation, the Grand Canyon, or an ant.

                     Like
washing less than nothing from your hands.

Station

Its back was leaves that mimed the leaves in back of us, but
the chair was painted white – white as the snow that never
stopped falling in my ears.
                                    The white leaves of the chair
that mocked the leaves of the backdrop, making us, for you,
the foredrop, imprinted leaf-prints on my bare back – white
ones.
    I held my gurgling sister in my lap, child whose cloud
I held as well, as the white wrought chair with its white leaves
sped us toward the sanctuary of damage.
                                    Can you, where you are
now, remember the garden chair I held her in for you?
                                                    We make
a crazy Pietà, my newborn sister and I.
                                    You step back.
                                                    In my
lap there rests a cloud of swaddling blankets like a shroud,
and on the cloud a laughing child.
                                    I squint and smile.
                                                    I'm round-
faced as a moon on a string, towheaded, slope-shouldered, vague
as a lamb and shorn like one.
                            The backdrop won't drop back
its ivied wall.

Station

I was teaching my little sister how to fly when she broke her arm.

    I did.

        I lay back in the snow and put my galoshes against her skinny butt and pushed her into the sky.

                    Over and over up-ward into the falling, and the fallen caught her, and her laughter spilled.

    We got it wrong one time and that was it.

                    I said, "Now, now."

    My mother's white station wagon disappeared into the snow on its way to the white hospital, and the volume turned up.

Right now a spring snow falls and sublimes.

                    The snowline retreats upward like a rising hem of sky.

                The snow is disappearing toward me.

The Giants of History

The little people behind the scenes are getting ugly.

They are seizing their own destiny.
                              They are plotting
crimes against the big people *in* the scenes.
                              They spite
the holy and the hoi polloi alike.
                              They've had enough
of us.
          The little people behind the scenes become tourists.

They want to meet other little people behind other scenes,
but their only friends are the giants of history, who are
no good to them now, in their hour of need.

Stories Are Made of Mistakes

I.

Even the pole bean tendrils sought out and gripped their
frames within six hours of my setting them.
                                    One of the things
that is breaking my heart is that I can't trust language to
express any thanks.
                        My pole beans, my honeybees, my coyotes,
my dog, all my good horses.

2.

The black mare I shouldn't have bought and bought, and once
I had, should have shipped, bucked me, too, the first time
I got up.
            But God she was a beauty.
                                    I thought if I just rode her
I could ride her down.
                        Her name was Sara and we kept it at that.

All she wanted to do was run.
                                    Ears back, flat out, nose pushed
into the next life.
                    I wanted her to learn to walk.

3.

After about a year of chop I turned her uphill on a good gravel
road and said, "ok, you bitch, you want to run?"
                                            I let go
her head and gave her the steel.

I'd never been on a horse so
fast.

I've never been on one since.

So fast you couldn't
count the beats in the rhythm of her gait.

Suicidal.

But when,
after some miles, she started to flag, I said, "I thought you
wanted to run," and dug her out again.

4.

The pole bean tendrils sought their frames within six hours
of my setting them.

They broke my heart.

They gripped.

5.

A patch of sunlight mottled the shade.

Whether she never
saw the root that snaked through the shadow or was just too
far in front of herself, I'll never know.

She stumbled
and fell.

First on her knees then over.

We rasped together
down the gravel road, black mare on top of me.

We rasped
to a halt.

She jumped to her feet.

She stared at me.

I
could see the bone in both her knees.

Ribbons of hide hanging.

Blood like volunteer firemen beginning to rise to the occasion.

6.

Ten years later, today, I'm riding her.
                                I keep her reined
in most of the time.
                        She tosses her head, snaps tie-downs.

She dances and whirls, doubles under and rears incessantly.

She makes me the butt of ridicule:
                                "So, uh, Jim, how old
is that mare?"
                "She must be twenty now."
                                        "Don't you think
it's time she was broke?"
                        Every once in a while I let her
run and break my heart.
                        Anyone watching stops breathing.

7.

If I ever get to heaven and know who I am, I'd like to over-
hear my daughter tell a story to her children.
                                        "Sometimes
my dad used to ride this black mare…"

Veronica

(See "Untitled, 1968," page 220)

Contraries and Opposites (Requestrian)

for Enja

When they blew up the building it went down in slow motion –
more like a ton of feathers than the bricks it was.
                                    When
you put down a horse she falls so hard no ton of bricks
could compare.
                    But if the horse is down, unable to rise,
like the brood mare who, with a two-month foal at her side,
breaks her leg above the hock because the cut-bank caved
and there was a root, the bullet sends her striving straight
into the air, failing to stand one last time.
                                    Then, without
dread or hint of bitterness, the foal noses her mother's
muzzle as more blood than you'd think was in a horse gushes
from the nostrils and the sandy earth accepts it all.
                                    The
filly, because this is no stranger than anything else she's
seen, as the last of the blood and the last of the breath
begin to froth and bubble, serenely sniffs.
                                    That's when
the muzzle of the rifle, its right work done, turns away.

But forget about that.
                    After the life drains and before
death grins through the mare (no absence but presence, I
swear) there is the sickening moment of nothing in between.

That space of nothing, not the rifle's report, makes the
filly bolt.

She comes back to sniff and snort when death is
safely in place.

She turns to look at you as if to say what's
next?

Station

Now that Hell is frozen over a lot can happen.
                                                  Flat as
a bat, cold as gold, later than never, better than ever.

Everyone tells the blind man how great they think his
dog is.
          Life is short; it's the afternoon that's long.

Life is tiny as a mosquito's penis.
                                        The afternoon is
longer than anything God's got.
                                      But this is just the story
of a small discussion group gone wrong.
                                              The topic was
supposed to be:
          Who needs the moon?
                                    Then someone offered:

Anyone who thinks he knows is wrong.
                                          Another countered:

It's really hard to stay alive for a lifetime.
                                              So
rollicky and impecunious.
                            The small discussion group
gone wrong hits the streets walking six or seven abreast.

They hector innocent passersby.
                                  They bypass no one.
                                                        I
can't guess, but they know why.

                    They can't squint the
church into a picture.
                    Old moon stalks the ridgetop.

By the time it's all over the small discussion group agrees
to blow up everything with a shoebox full of snow.

Strip

1.

His name was really Eros, bastard son of a rural whore.

His
schizophrenia was ascribable, if you will, to being locked
in a room most of his childhood while his mother plied her
trade.

One day unknowing I gave her a lift as she thumbed
into town.

She stunned the air just like a stagnant pond.

2.

The first time I met Eros he was a little too close and he
was leering at my wife.

Had I been Umbrian I would have done
differently.

Where I come from people don't ask for it like
that.

I asked him to excuse us.

He leered on.

I excused him.

He leered on.

3.

After that he followed my wife whenever she went out alone.

"Don't fret," the townspeople cooed, "He's just one of our
crazies.

We have to learn to accommodate them.

Il Signore

would have it so.

Occasionally he strikes someone. It's

no big deal."

And so it was.

And so it ever was.

4.

At Midnight Mass the church was packed with peasantry and
gentry, furs and motley.

Eros stood close behind me.

I

overheard him tell his mother, "It's all right.

You are as

good as them.

In His eyes, better.

Take communion, Mamma.

Come on, I'll lead you."

He took her by the hand and led her

forward.

5

That summer, ten-year-old Maria Magdalena Fortunati, who
had saved and saved all year for a pair of swimming goggles,
put them on for the first time and leapt into the public
pool.

Now she could see clearly through the stingy water.

What she saw when she looked down was Eros drowned, so clear
at first she disbelieved that liquid, fishlike, human form,
that fleshy sigh splayed there, face down.

Velut maris stella.

Parens et puella.
No one rolled bones for his clothes, I'll wager.

Objectivity Is Abjectivity

I burn in hope of finding fuel. There's more of me where I
come from.

              I'd ask Jesus to help me but it always seems like
he's the one who needs the help.

                        The worst is over but the best
has been over for a long time.

                     The invisible is indivisible:
God the thought that through us moves toward feeling.

                                 He
disappeared out of nowhere, so uncreated.

                        Since crucifixion
was commonplace then, they must have had specialists.

                              Carpenters
expert in mortise and tenon, guys who could really sink a nail
through an open hand with confidence.

                       Christ, the carpenter,
must have known how good his cross, his crucifier.

                            I can
tell you it feels good to drive a nail.

                     An open hand, if you
were used to it, would be no obstacle.

                   God the thought that
through us moves toward feeling.

Kiwi Blake

Birds that cut the airy way are five times closed to all
in me that dies.

        I'm willing to accept all things unknown
and try to see as much as possible.

            I'm OK with missing most
of it by eye.

        My sister in New Zealand says I have to see
the Southern Cross before I die.

Station

I envy the soldiers' sleep – ah, the sleep of a soldier.

Jesus was laid in the tomb and rocked in.
                              The good luck of
the soldier sleeping through what he was never meant to see.

The day before, when Jesus "died on the cross," was the day
he harrowed heaven.
                    No one was there.
                              It was just a big desert
like the Great Basin where the rain that falls finds no river,
where the rain has nowhere to go but back.
                              Jesus plowed the
sand behind his best donkey, but even in sand the plow would
not scour.
           His harrow raised apparitions of dust: a wedding
dress, a suit of Spanish armor, a cassock, a twisted sword,
Judas warming his hands by a dusty fire.
                              But really, there
was no one.
           No, no one.

NOTES

The last line of "Rintrah Roars" is from Porchia.

The poem "Veronica" originally appeared in *Lethal Frequencies* as "Untitled, 1968," but was written as a part of the "Stations" series.

The poem "Small Countries" is page 131 from *The Meadow*, by James Galvin (Henry Holt, 1992).

ABOUT THE AUTHOR

JAMES GALVIN's previous collections of poetry include *Lethal Frequencies* (Copper Canyon Press, 1995); *Imaginary Timber* (Doubleday, 1980); *God's Mistress* (1984 National Poetry Series winner, Harper & Row); and *Elements* (Copper Canyon Press, 1988). He has been the recipient of fellowships from the National Endowment for the Arts, the Lila Wallace–Reader's Digest Foundation, the Ingram–Merrill Foundation, and the Guggenheim Foundation. He has recently taught at the University of Montana and at the Iowa Writers' Workshop, and lives in Tie Siding, Wyoming.

BOOK DESIGN and composition by John D. Berry and Jennifer Van West, using Adobe Pagemaker 6.0 on a Macintosh 11vx and a Power 120. The type is Janson Text, a digital adaptation by Adrian Frutiger of the 17th-century type of Hungarian punchcutter Nicholas Kis. Kis spent ten years working in Amsterdam, and his type is one of the sturdy old-style typefaces typical of Dutch printing of the period. In the 20th century, it was adapted for hot-metal typesetting and widely used in fine books. The revived typeface was called "Janson" because it was mistakenly attributed at first to Anton Janson, a Dutch typographer who worked in Leipzig. Janson Text maintains many of the idiosyncracies of the original design and keeps its legibility at text sizes. *Printed by Malloy Lithographing.*